Lucius Lee Hubbard

Summer Vacations at Moosehead Lake and Vicinity

A practical Guide-Book for Tourists

Lucius Lee Hubbard

Summer Vacations at Moosehead Lake and Vicinity
A practical Guide-Book for Tourists

ISBN/EAN: 9783337143336

Printed in Europe, USA, Canada, Australia, Japan

Cover: Foto ©Lupo / pixelio.de

More available books at **www.hansebooks.com**

SUMMER VACATIONS

AT

MOOSEHEAD LAKE

AND VICINITY.

A Practical Guide-Book for Tourists:

DESCRIBING ROUTES FOR THE CANOE-MAN OVER THE PRINCIPAL
WATERS OF NORTHERN MAINE, WITH HINTS TO CAMPERS,
AND ESTIMATES OF EXPENSE FOR TOURS.

*Illustrated with Views of Penobscot and Kennebec Scenery, and
accompanied by a large Map of the Headwaters of the
Penobscot, Kennebec, and St. John Rivers.*

BY LUCIUS L. HUBBARD.

BOSTON:
A. WILLIAMS AND COMPANY.
1880.

Copyright, 1880,
BY LUCIUS L. HUBBARD.

Illustrations by Connelly & Co., Boston.

TO THE

Friends and Companions

WHO HAVE SHARED WITH HIM THE PLEASURES OF CAMPING OUT
IN THE WOODS OF MAINE,

THE AUTHOR

AFFECTIONATELY DEDICATES THIS LITTLE VOLUME,

IN THE EARNEST HOPE THAT, EVEN IF IT SHOULD CONTAIN
NOTHING NEW TO THEM, IT WILL AT LEAST SERVE
TO RECALL BRIGHT MEMORIES OF DAYS
THAT ARE PAST.

INTRODUCTION.

To the care-worn business man and overworked student, no relaxation from the constant wear of their respective callings is so grateful as that which comes while camping in the woods. "The accompaniments of life are removed, and selfishness, ambition, and care have here no place; a man is most truly thrown upon his own resources. To be alone with nature, without book, without work, without care, without the slightest hindrance to wandering at your own sweet will, with a heart which beats 'true to the kindred points of heaven and home,' and to be for this purpose in the very heart of the Moosehead forests, is more than all the trout-fishing, and almost the rival of the matchless views which meet the eye."* In the wild woods life is regenerated, and even after two weeks of camping out and canoeing one issues forth with renewed strength for the work of the coming year. Rest and recreation are an absolute necessity. A celebrated jurist of this country, no longer living, used to say he could do a year's work in ten months, but not in twelve.

* Rev. Julius H. Ward, in Harper's Magazine, August, 1875.

It then becomes a practical question, how deep into the forests must one penetrate with his birch-canoe to find this seclusion and relaxation, and what are the means of attaining them?

The advantage to canoe-men of having some definite and tangible information concerning the different lakes and water-courses over which their routes may take them, is too well known by those persons who have camped out in the woods of Maine to need proof. It often happens that the tourist comes to a part of a stream where the difficulty of further progress seems insurmountable. After successful efforts made to overcome the obstacles which first appeared, others take their place, and the chain seems unending. The luckless canoe-man in ignorance turns back disappointed, and seeks an easier route elsewhere, when, if he had but known it, smooth water and a picturesque and attractive course lay before him, within easy reach.

With a knowledge of this need, gained by experience, the writer has prepared the following pages for the benefit of *habitués* of Moosehead Lake, and of others who may have in view a visit to some of the wilder localities in its vicinity. The brevity necessarily required in a pocket guide-book has caused him to set forth facts without any attempt at embellishment, — plain, statistical facts, whose only function is to be useful. The book, aside from its illustrations, is not meant to be entertaining, and they who seek in its pages any elaborate or detailed descriptions of scenery will be disappointed.

That part of the work devoted to camping is also merely an epitome. Many topics touched upon had to be passed over briefly, and left perhaps incomplete, while others of scarcely less importance had to be omitted altogether. The information and advice actually given is, moreover, very much condensed, and, such as it is, the writer offers it to beginners in the art of camping, as a stepping-stone to a more extended knowledge, which can best be obtained by experience.

He who goes into the woods to camp for the first time will be at a loss to understand many of the phrases in vogue among older campers and guides, some few of which, on account of their brevity, have been used in the following pages. The word "pitch" refers either to the resinous mixture used on canoes, to a small water-fall, or to the height of a stream. After a hard rain one may say, "There is a good pitch of water." "Rips" is a word used of a stretch of water, which is not long enough nor rough enough to be called "rapids." To "drop" a canoe over a "pitch" is to let it float over it, the canoe-man guiding it from the shore with a setting-pole, and with the "painter," or leading-rope.

A "landing" is a term used by lumbermen to denote a place cleared of bushes and trees on the bank of a stream or pond, to which the logs cut in winter are hauled, in anticipation of the spring floods.

"Logon," probably a derivative of "lagoon," means a very shallow arm of a stream or pond, where lilies and grass grow profusely.

"Wangen" is a shelter-tent, one might say, made of bark or boughs, and is perhaps oftenest used by "river-drivers" in the spring, when engaged in floating or "driving" logs down the rivers to market.

In the vicinity of Moosehead Lake the expressions "East Branch," "West Branch," "North Branch" and "South Branch" refer to the Penobscot River. Moreover, the North and South Branches are actually branches of the West Branch.

On the Kennebec "The Forks" means the junction of that river with Dead River.

The term "navigation" as used in the following pages refers to canoes, and readers will also note the difference between the right and left *banks* of a stream, and the same terms without the word "bank."

The distances given are only approximate, but are founded on close observation and studied comparison.

No changes have been made in the text of this, the second edition, which is published separately from the map which accompanied the first edition; woodcuts have been substituted for photographic reproductions, and the book is offered to the public with the wish that it may prove a useful and serviceable companion to campers-out in the woods of Northern Maine.

The author again acknowledges his grateful appreciation to Dr. Elliott Coues, U. S. A., for the use, kindly and promptly granted, of his Hygienic Notes, and to many other obliging persons for timely and important information and assistance.

CAMBRIDGE, *June* 10, 1880.

LIST OF ILLUSTRATIONS.

	PAGE
Mount Kineo from Kineo Cove	*Frontispiece*
Mouth of Spencer Brook	18
Mount Kineo — Pebble Beach	32
Mount Kineo — Table Rock	48
Socatean Falls and Pool	60
Chesuncook Lake	64
Ripogenus Gorge — Looking East	68
Ripogenus Gorge — Looking West	70
Millinokett Lake	76
Moxie Falls	122

MAPS.

Moosehead Lake and Vicinity	38
Caucomgomoc Lake and Vicinity	96

CONTENTS.

PART FIRST.
How to Camp Out.

	PAGE
Time of Year	1
Number in a Party	2
A Camper's Outfit, — Where and How to Get it	3
Camp "Kit"	4
Personal Luggage	7
Provisions	14
Canoes and their Usage	16
Guides	19
Camp-Ground	22
Camp-Fire	24
Cooking	25
Dressing Game	28
Hygienic Notes	29

PART SECOND.
Moosehead Lake and Immediate Vicinity.

Routes from Boston to Moosehead Lake	39
Moosehead Lake	44
Mount Kineo	48

Tours beyond Moosehead Lake.

	PAGE
West Branch of the Penobscot, — Going Down	62
Jo Mary and Neighboring Lakes	76
Northwest Carry	77
West Branch of the Penobscot, — Seeboomook Falls	78
West Branch of the Penobscot, — Going Up	79
South Branch of the Penobscot	82
North Branch of the Penobscot	86
St. John Pond and Baker Lake	91
Caucomgomoc Lake	93
Allagash Lake	100
Down the St. John River	101
East Branch of the Penobscot	107
Ebeeme Ponds and Pleasant River	109
Katahdin Iron-Works	111
Sebec Lake	112
Mount Katahdin from the East	115
Forks of the Kennebec and Vicinity	117
Moose River above Moose River Village	126
Game and Fish of Northern Maine	129
Digest of Game and Fish Laws	132
Tables of Tours for Campers	135
Expense of Tours	138
Advertisements	140
Index	141

SUMMER VACATIONS

AT

MOOSEHEAD LAKE.

PART FIRST.
HOW TO CAMP OUT.

TIME OF YEAR.

ALL seasons have their respective advantages for the hunter or trapper, whether sportsman or not, according to the object he has in view. Each has its own disadvantages as well, but for general purposes of camping-out September and October offer the most attractions and have the fewest drawbacks. Black-flies and mosquitoes have then ceased their torments, the weather is apt to be settled and pleasant, the nights cool, and game is in its prime, and likely to be found everywhere.

The best fishing is undoubtedly to be had — at least in places of most frequent resort — in early spring, just after the ice breaks up in the lakes and streams. The larger game frequents the feeding-grounds on the banks of streams, and shores of ponds, and comes down to the water at night, in the hot weather of midsummer. But these are the halcyon days of the black-fly and mosquito, the one a constant attendant by day, and the other by night, both combining to make life miserable for the reckless sportsman. Besides, the days are sweltering and the nights oppressive.

Midwinter is not without its attraction, — principally that of novelty for him who ventures into the woods too far north. He is soon disabused of the fascination which drew him thither, and learns that it is much more comfortable to put up at some hotel or cabin at the outskirts of civilization, and to make hunting excursions on snow-shoes from these, and to fish through the ice under cover of a warm little fish-house, than to camp under a shelter tent with the snow four feet deep around him, and the mercury at twenty-five below zero.

NUMBER IN A PARTY.

The number of persons of which a party should consist will depend more or less on the characteristics of the individuals and the object in view. Travelling — especially in the woods — is apt to show up the least amiable side of one's disposition, and the larger the party, the more difficult will it be to have united counsels and action. If you are bent on having a jolly time, and are not particular about getting game and fish, nor where you go, you can well join a large party; but when you go mainly for the enjoyments of hunting and fishing such as can only be had in the wild woods, go with one friend, — a tried friend, on whose good sense and unselfishness you can rely. The next best way, and you may prefer it, is to go alone, with a trusty and competent guide. Two men, each with a canoe and guide, is an advantageous combination, for the pairs can separate for a time, if advisable, and occupy different grounds near together. For a short trip two men and one guide can go in one canoe, but for a trip of two weeks or more a canoe will only hold two men and luggage, and will have an ample load at that.

A CAMPER'S OUTFIT, — WHERE AND HOW TO GET IT.

As Mr. Gould has happily suggested in his interesting book, "How to Camp Out," you should begin to make preparations for your trip two or three months before you intend to start. To make small purchases of useful articles to be taken with you, and to dwell in anticipation on what is before you, affords almost as much pleasure as the later enjoyment of the woods. There is great satisfaction in picturing to yourself what part this and that article will play in your adventures, or in what sort of a place, whether lake or brook, mountain or meadow, it will first be called into requisition. Then, too, if you put off all preparation until the last moment, you may forget some of the most important parts of your outfit, — a *sine qua non*, — and the thought of what "might have been" will be quite aggravating. Collect your outfit, piece by piece; appropriate a closet or a trunk to its exclusive use, and put the parts of your collection into it, day by day, keeping a list from which to check off each item as soon as obtained. Every time an article suggests itself to you as one that is likely to be indispensable, get it. Only be careful to make your load as light as possible. Remember that what one may consider a necessity at home may be regarded as a luxury in the woods, and that to carry one pound of extra weight fifty miles is equivalent to carrying fifty pounds one mile.

Get everything you need, in the way of personal luggage, at home. You seldom have time or inclination to stop over, by the way, and are not at all sure to find what you want at the last village on the verge of the forest. By "personal luggage" the writer means everything exclusive of food, and of the camp "kit," a term explained below.

It is very convenient, if you mean to use canned goods in the woods, to have them packed at home, in a box with rope handles on each end of it, and to take them with you as luggage.

CAMP "KIT."

Parties who go into camp with guides do not usually have to provide what is termed the "kit." This includes, besides canoe and tent, axes, cooking utensils, and the like, — articles which nearly all guides own in quantities sufficient for parties of two or three.

For persons who may be about to go into camp without guides, the following list of articles will be found useful, if not indispensable : —

Party of Two.	Party of Four.
Axe, one ; 3¼ lbs.	two.
Baker, small	medium.
Breadpan ; 2 qts.	3 qts.
Butter-box, wooden	
Can-opener	
Coffee-pot ; 1 qt.	2 qts.

Forks, three	five.
Firkins, or bags, for provisions	
Frying-pans, two, medium	two, large.
Kettle, iron; 2 qts.	3 qts.
Knives, three	five.
Molasses-can; 1 gal.	
Mop for dishes	
Pepper-shaker	
Pitch dipper, — handle riveted	two.
Potato bag	
Rope for canoe, — "Painter"	
Salt-shaker	
Sponge for canoe	two.
Spoon, one, large	
Teaspoons, three	six.
Tent (A) 7ft. × 8ft.	
Tin dippers, four	six.
Tin pails; two, 2 qts.	three, 3 qts.
Tin plates, four	six.

For parties of more than four persons, the capacity of the pails, pots, and pans will have to be proportionally larger, and the number of the more necessary table-dishes increased, so that there will be two or three extra of each kind.

The cost of an outfit for two, such as is given above, will be about fifteen dollars, exclusive of tent, which may be bought for ten or twelve dollars.

Of course, persons *can* get along with fewer things than those above enumerated. The hunter often goes into the woods, in midwinter, and his outfit consists of a thin blanket, an axe, rifle, sheath-knife, frying-pan, and large tin dipper. With these, a bag of flour, a piece of pork, and what he shoots, he sustains himself, and makes no complaint. In like manner, a camper's "kit" can be crude, or elaborate, to suit his whims or his pocket; and he can direct his outlay in such a manner as to undergo a greater or less degree of "roughing it," — and to his entire satisfaction.

For the benefit of parties who go to Moosehead Lake, it may be well to say that all of the above articles can be bought at Greenville, except bags for provisions, which will have to be brought from home. These should be strong, made of stout drilling, and of various sizes, according to the bulk of the articles meant to be carried in them. Moreover, a large canvas bag, or rubber navy bag, should make part of the kit, to hold the smaller bags, and keep their contents dry.

It has been, and still is, quite common to carry provisions into the woods in wooden buckets or firkins. They answer very well for trips where little or no carrying is to be done, but are very much of a nuisance when the contrary is the case. The principal advantage in having bags is, that, as fast as your food is consumed, the *bulk* of your luggage decreases, which with buckets is not appreciable. *One* bucket, for dishes, salt and pepper shakers, can-opener, condensed milk, and other odds and ends, will more than compensate, in convenience, the trouble of carrying it. Axes and hatchets should be provided with some sort of cover. They are then less troublesome and harmful, and can be thrown into a canoe or on shore without danger, either of cutting something else, or of being themselves nicked or dulled. They can also be carried safely in one's belt, over carries and through the woods.

One or two kettle-holders will prove extremely useful, and easy to carry; a small whetstone and a crooked knife, too, may well be added to the kit.

An iron bean-pot will be found a great luxury, if it does not have to be "carried" much. Otherwise take *canned* beans.

A farina boiler, which consists of two pails, the smaller set in the other, serves well to cook oat-meal and mush, without risk of burning, — either the food or the cook.

A shelter tent is warmer than an A tent, if a fire is kept blazing before it all night, but it is otherwise less convenient, especially in stormy weather.

PERSONAL LUGGAGE.

The writer first began to camp out ten years ago. His preparations for his initial trip to the woods were crude. As beginners, we do not feel the need of many things, which want of experience, perhaps as much as lack of means, prevents us from getting; but after a series of summers spent in the woods, we learn how we can, in many ways, add materially to our enjoyment and comfort, at trifling expense, and with only a slight addition to the weight of our luggage.

Following is a list of articles the writer deems essential to a tolerable degree of comfort and ease, while out for a two weeks' canoeing excursion : —

> One pair stout shoes, well greased.
> One pair stout slippers.
> One suit, — old, but stout clothes.
> One extra pair pantaloons (Scotch goods).
> Two woollen shirts with collars.
> One change of under-clothes.
> Slouch felt hat (gray).
> Two or three pairs heavy woollen socks.
> Two silk handkerchiefs.

A cardigan jacket (dark gray).
A light rubber coat.
Two rubber blankets, — for each person.
One pair heavy woollen blankets, — for each person.
A blanket strap.
Two carrying straps.
Court and sticking plaster.
Small flask of brandy.
Bottle Jamaica ginger.
Box of grease for boots.
Bottle of mosquito mixture.
Piece of soap in small tin-box.
Sponge, tooth-brush, comb, and two towels.
Camp candlestick and candles.
Two or three haversacks, or a knapsack.
Mosquito net for the head.
A knit cap for sleeping.
Pieces of rope and twine.
Rags, and a small bottle of gun-oil.
Needles, thread, beeswax, and a small awl.
Compass, matches.
Broad belt, with strap for attaching tin cup.
Good sheath-knife.
Cartridge-box (old army cap-box).
Allen, or Winchester, rifle, and from 50 to 100 cartridges.
Cheap fly-rod, four leaders, and a dozen flies.
Six stout hooks.
Reel, and fifty yards oiled-silk line.
Pack of cards — for rainy days.
Pocket-map of region to be visited.

COMMENTS ON THE FOREGOING.

Do not wear boots into the woods. They are cumbersome, and sure to get wet, and when in that condition are very hard to get off and on. A pair of loose-fitting brogans, such as can be bought for about two dollars, or an old pair of Waukenphast's shoes, if you have them, will be found most comfortable. Shoes should fit snugly, without pinching. If your feet are going to be out of order for want of proper covering, you would better go back home at once. A piece of leather may prove of service in your "kit." The writer has of late years found rubber boots, which come up half-way between knee and hip, almost indispensable where wading is necessary. However, a pair of stout shoes, well greased, will answer the purpose, and when you return to camp with wet feet, the comfort of dry socks and slippers will be exceedingly grateful. If you take rubber boots, a change of pantaloons will not be necessary.

An excellent substitute for heavy shoes and slippers will be found in moccasons, which when new are waterproof, and fit the foot easily. They are good either in a canoe, or when on the walk; an extra sole on the inside helps to protect the foot from roots and stones. In this connection, when you dry your shoes or moccasons, be careful not to expose them to too great heat. Greased leather, or the fatty hide of any animal, will, when exposed to the sun, or to a hot fire, burn very quickly, and before one would suspect it. It is a serious thing to lose one's foot-covering in the woods.

A heavy coat, or overcoat, will be found to be an incumbrance from its weight, and inconvenient when paddling. A good cardigan jacket and a thick vest will be all the extra clothing needed for cold days in September. The suit one wears should be such as one does not expect to use again. Scotch goods are preferable, as they dry easily after a wetting. Their color should be dark gray, if possible, to resemble that of the trunks of the trees. The wearer will thus be less likely to attract the notice of game that may come in his way.

A pair of suspenders is a comfort one should not be without. It does not matter if they do not look well over your woollen shirt.

A light rubber coat in the woods is invaluable, and two or three extra rubber blankets are apt to be quite serviceable, in more ways than one. Should a shower overtake you *en route*, one of them thrown over your canoe-load protects it thoroughly. In camp two of them stretched overhead on either side of a horizontal pole make a good shelter both for your table and luggage, and they also make a warm covering to sleep under, on cold nights.

A good substitute for tent, and rubber blankets too, consists in pieces of cotton cloth, 7ft. × 4ft., soaked in boiled linseed-oil. If made with eyelet-holes in the margin, they will answer the purpose of a tent, four of them being laced together in pairs, two side to side, and these pairs end to end. The two ends thus laced together are laid on the ridge-pole of the tent, and triangular pieces buttoned on at each end complete the dwelling.

One pair of stout uncut woollen blankets for each person is none too many. For cold nights in September more warmth and comfort can be had by having your blankets doubled over and sewed up on one *end*, and three quarters up the side, like a bag, so that when in it you have two thicknesses of blanket over and under you, and your feet cannot become uncovered during sleep. The top of the blanket can, if necessary, be drawn up over the head, while that part of the side left unsewed will furnish a good breathing-place.

Leather carrying-straps consist of a *centre piece* about a foot long and two inches wide, firmly sewed, at either extremity, to slightly tapering *end pieces* ten feet long and half an inch wide.

To make a pack, spread out on the ground your blanket, tent, or whatever you intend to use for the purpose, and double it over, more or less, to suit the size of your load. One or two trials will enable you to judge accurately of the extent of covering needed for the pack. Lay the strap on the blanket, &c., so that the *centre piece* shall be just over the edge of it, opposite the middle of the side, and the *end pieces* shall extend from the same side along the ends of the blanket, half-way from the middle of it to the ends. Then fold the ends of the blanket over the strap, letting them meet in the middle, or overlap, if necessary. The foundation of your pack is now ready. Make a pile of your luggage, buckets, provisions, &c. on the blanket, and when you think you have weight or bulk enough, take the ends of your strap, one at a time, and knot each to the corresponding end of the *centre piece;* pull tightly, so that the ends of your blanket will be drawn together like the mouth of a bag. After the knots shall have been made, bring the ends of your strap together at the middle of the pack under the *centre piece*, cross them and carry them around to the opposite side of the pack, where they shall be firmly and finally knotted. The pack thus made is slung on the back; the broad part of the strap rests against the forehead, and by leaning forward, and holding the strap with both hands over the shoulders, a heavy weight can be carried with comparative ease. The Indians use this method almost altogether.

The foregoing list includes a small quantity of brandy. This should be used only in case of sickness. People are supposed to go into the woods for the purpose of gaining health and strength, and this inestimable privilege should not be prostituted by the use of liquor, merely to gratify an appetite for drink. The use of stimulants is sure to be followed by an unhealthy reaction, and in the woods, if nowhere else, there ought to be enough in Nature's charms to draw one away from a practice at once ruinous to health and to self-respect. For colds, or after a wetting of the body, Jamaica ginger will be found an excellent remedy and preventive.

Parties who camp out in July or August will need some mosquito-repellent, to put on their faces and hands. Various compounds are put up, and are for sale, by druggists and others, which may answer the purpose; but the writer has never found anything better than oil of tar, and sweet oil or glycerine, in equal quantities, and a little gum camphor and oil of pennyroyal mixed with it. At first, renewed applications are necessary at short intervals, until the skin becomes moist, and saturated with the odor of the mixture.

For ladies, a pair of thick buckskin gauntlets, and a good veil, are the best and most pleasant substitutes for the above mixture.

A mosquito net for the head, such as are for sale at sporting emporiums, will be a great comfort on warm nights, and especially about daybreak.

Matches should be kept in a small tight tin box, in a dry part of your luggage. A water-proof pocket-match-box you should always carry with you, well filled. You may need it once in ten years, but might fare badly that one time if caught without matches.

As to gun and fishing-tackle, some prefer one kind and some another. Usually campers-out take just what they can conveniently get. The Winchester gun, eight-shooter, is now the favorite. It is cheap, reliable, and can be fired and reloaded from the shoulder, besides being of a desirable weight. The Allen gun is also a good gun for a cheap one, but, not having a magazine, cannot be fired so rapidly as the Winchester. For a two weeks' trip fifty cartridges will be found more than enough, unless one expects to ignore the possible presence of large game, and to shoot right and left at anything which may furnish a good target.

A shot-gun will generally be found a useless encumbrance.

For fly rods, one made of ash and lancewood, and which weighs from eight to twelve ounces, and costs about five dollars, will answer well enough for ordinary fishing. Higher-priced rods can be had according to one's taste and resources, and afford, perhaps, more satisfaction to the scientific fisherman. They can well be taken care of, when the owner is at a hotel, but the camper-out will find it rather irksome to be continually putting his rod together, and taking it apart to avoid a rain-storm or the dews of night.

For flies, the best are the Montreal, red-ibis, brown-hackle, and blue-jay. For spring-fishing additional varieties may be found good, such as the Jenny-Lind, the grizzle-king, the professor, and the gray-drake.

Six-foot leaders are long enough. They should be of a pale bluish tint.

A map is desirable as a guide; it also serves to while away many an hour which might otherwise be dull. You become familiar with the character of the country, and, after study of the different water-courses, can often plan out trips, and post yourself upon their practicability, by questioning guides and others, whenever opportunity offers.

PROVISIONS.

The following list of provisions will be found to contain all that is necessary for good camp-fare, together with a little that may be regarded as a luxury. The acid in pickles, tomatoes, and dried or canned fruit, serves as a corrective to the large amount of fat unavoidably eaten by campers, and just enough of these articles should be taken to serve this purpose, and vary one's diet, without adding too much extra weight to the necessary canoe-load.

The fractions opposite each article in the list represent the amount of such article which a man of average "camp-appetite" will eat in one day, and are based on the writer's experience with ten different men on six different trips. To know approximately how much to take for a given time, it is hardly necessary to say, multiply the number in your party by the number of days you are to be in camp, and this result by the several fractions. Of course there can be no absolute gauge of appetites, and during the last few days of your trip you may have to live on short rations; or you may find so much game as to have an overplus of provisions. In either case, however, this list will be found to be not wide of the mark.

	Daily Amount per Person.
Baking powder	1-15 box.
Beans	1-16 qt., or 1-12 can.
Butter	1-12 lb.
Chocolate	1-30 lb.
Coffee	1-45 lb.
Condensed milk	7-100 can.
Corn	1-20 can.
Corned beef	1-12 lb.
Dried peaches	1-20 lb.
Flour, white and Graham	1-2 lb.
Hard bread	3-20 lb.
Lard	1-10 lb.
Molasses	1-30 qt.
Oat meal, Cracked wheat, Pearled barley	2-25 lb.
Onions	1-20 lb.
Pepper	1-150 lb.
Pickles	optional.
Potatoes	1-75 bu.
Pork or bacon	1-4 lb.
Salt	1-25 lb.
Sugar	6-25 lb.
Sugar, maple	optional.
Tea	1-150 lb.
Tomatoes	1-12 can.

It must be borne in mind that, if any one of the above articles is not taken, more of something else must be substituted. Maple sugar, dried or canned fruit, chocolate, and corned beef are luxuries, and will have to be used sparingly, if taken in the quantities given above. Canned meats will be found most acceptable for lunch, when you are on the move and do not or cannot stop long enough to cook. Flour will generally be found preferable to hard bread, as the latter is apt to become crumbled on being moved from place to place.

Some parties go into the woods with a notion that they are sure to get all the game they need for subsistence, and that it is therefore unnecessary to take more than enough flour, &c. to give a pleasant change to one's diet. This is a great mistake. Rely on your own larder, not on Nature's, and you will be much better off.

CANOES AND THEIR USAGE.

A good birch-canoe should be made of tough bark, the eyes of which are not easily broken, and there should not be any inequalities or "humps" on that part which is usually in the water, for the water by swelling them makes the "humps" more prominent, and thus more likely to be scraped or broken by contact with rocks. Nor should a canoe be what is vulgarly called "hog-backed," that is, lower in the middle than at the ends. For general use it should be flat-bottomed, rather than have a slight keel. It will then ride in shallower water, and be less ticklish and more manageable.

One can, with a little practice, learn how to *paddle* a canoe; the secret of keeping a straight course lies in feathering the paddle at the end of the stroke. To be able to use the *setting-pole* skilfully requires more study, not only to learn the effect on the canoe of each position and movement of the pole, but also the additional effect on it of the current or "set" of the water, and of gusts of wind, all of which must be "compensated."

At all times a canoe should be so loaded as to be "trim," or perfectly level. A slight displacement of equlibrium is very annoying.

When poling through rapids, the chief points to be borne in mind are to keep the bow pretty well loaded (more so when going up than when coming down), and to *keep it pointed in a line parallel with the current.* In sinking the pole into the water, it should be held away from the side of the canoe, and in pushing laterally it should be used from that side towards which you wish the bow to go. Much less strength is needed to *push* the bow around in this way, than to *pull* it around from the other side, besides which it is much less dangerous. In the latter case the current may swing the stern against and over the pole, and the jar and pressure may send the canoe-man into the water, or make him drop his pole. You should stand erect in the stern, with the left foot in front, and both feet on a line with the length of the canoe. Grasp the pole with both hands, the right uppermost, so that on the end of the push the left will be free to take hold higher up. This position is for poling on the right side. The pole may be shifted from side to side, and either end used, as emergency requires, but the end that is shod with a pick is alone reliable among slippery rocks.

The posture of the man in the stern of a canoe is usually sitting on the rear thwart and rails behind it.

The bow-man's best position is kneeling on the bottom, his thighs supported by the second thwart. More work can be done in this position than if sitting on the thwart or on a seat behind it, although the latter is the more comfortable. The more lightly a canoe is loaded, the more easily it can be overturned, and for this reason it is best for both the bow-man and stern-man to *sit on the bottom* of the canoe while on stormy water.

The scope of this work will not admit of more general discussion of this topic. A little practice, and a wetting or two, will give one sufficient insight into the theory to enable one soon to be quite at home in a canoe.

For leaks in the canoe a mixture of resin, and tallow or other fresh grease, is generally used. A small quantity of grease is needed, more or less, according as the water is cold or warm. If your mixture should be too soft, boiling will make it harder. It can be tested by putting a few drops on a chip, and dipping it in the water. The bark must be quite dry when it is applied, which condition is best produced by turning over the canoe and exposing it to the sun, or by holding a fire-brand near the injured part. And in this connection it may be said, that a canoe, when not required for use, should always be taken out of the water and turned over. While afloat, its bark becomes saturated with water, and increases very much in weight.

For the same reason, do not get sand into your canoe. It gets down under the ribs, and cannot be removed. Wash off the soles of your shoes before you step in, and do not step in when by so doing your

MOUTH OF SPENCER BROOK.

canoe will be depressed on to sharp rocks or gravel. This rubs the bark and makes the eyes crack. A canoe should be treated as carefully as if it were made of glass.

If you should unfortunately get out of pitch, and have a leaky canoe, look for a large pine-tree, and cut a small horizontal trough in one side of it, about three or four inches deep, into which the resinous sap will run. Boil this down to the proper consistency, add grease, and apply hot with a small flat stick. If you have not time to do this, a substitute for pitch may be found in spruce-gum.

It is dangerous to attempt to sail in a canoe. When your course is straight, you can sometimes profitably lash two canoes together, not so close that they will chafe, and, by means of a rubber blanket or coat, sail before the wind. In a single canoe a thick bush planted or held in the bow will greatly help to accelerate your speed before the wind.

It may not be out of place to say here, never allow the man in the stern of a canoe to have a loaded gun by his side while you are in the bow. The reason is too obvious to need explanation.

GUIDES.

Well-informed and reliable guides can be secured at prices ranging from one to two and a half dollars a day, according to the locality, and according to the length and difficulty of the trip in view. At Moosehead Lake, for services rendered parties staying at any of the hotels on the lake, the regular price is two dollars and a half and board, or three dollars, the guide to "find" himself. For services from Moosehead on a trip where a canoe is likely to receive hard usage, three dollars per day and board may be asked, while for a long and not difficult trip less than two and a half dollars and board may be reasonable compensation.

Away from Moosehead Lake, guide-hire is rarely more than two dollars a day, while at the Forks of the Kennebec and at Sebec Lake good guides may be had for from a dollar to a dollar and a half a day, and board.

The laws of supply and demand apply to guides and their compensation, as well as to other marketable "commodities," and *good* guides in the "season" are apt to have little spare time on their hands to dispose of at less than the usual local rates. Inferior guides, lacking in knowledge of the various routes and fishing grounds, can be had at a very low price.

Guides who receive the above-named prices furnish a canoe and the necessary camp "kit," except blankets. Sportsmen provide all the food needed.

Cases have been not uncommon where men of prominence in their own neighborhood have knowingly recommended as competent guides persons of notoriously bad character, temper, or incapacity. Again, some guides have wilfully imposed upon parties engaging them, and by misrepresentation, apathy, or opposition to their wishes, have made an utter failure of what could otherwise have been a delightful trip,— one on which perhaps the participants had been building hopes of pleasure for months previously. Such practices do great injury to those guides who conscientiously try to make their employers realize their expectations of a pleasant vacation, and are apt to reflect on the entire fraternity, to their great discredit.*

In this connection it may not be out of place to say a word about the treatment of guides. They may picture in exaggerated language the hardships of this or that particular trip, and dwell upon the advantages of some others, which they well know will require much less labor on their part. You thus may be imposed upon, and may miss having a great deal of enjoyment. Get your information well digested before you start, and when your mind is once made up, push ahead. Let your guide understand, at the outset, where you mean to go, and that you expect him to devote all his energy and experience to getting there.

On the other hand, do not harass him in trivial matters. Some persons stand over a guide, when he is cooking, and object to this way of holding the frying-pan, or that way of turning the flippers, and perhaps in a majority of cases thoughtlessly annoy him when there is no necessity for it.

Give your guide plenty of time to select a good camp-ground, and to prepare for the night. Favor him when you can. Keep your end of the canoe trim, and do not hesitate to get out and walk now and then, if by so doing you can avoid tearing or scraping the bark.

* Visitors at Moosehead Lake can obtain reliable information about guides, from the superintendent of the Mt. Kineo House, and excursionists will do well, in all cases, to engage their guides a month in advance.

CAMP-GROUND.

It is of the utmost importance for tourists to stop early enough, at the end of each day, to select a good site for their camp, to pitch their tent, and to get wood enough together to last over night. Many people do not seem to think how hard it is to do all of these things in the dark. Only an absolute necessity should induce late camping. An hour before sunset is late enough to cease paddling.

A good camp-ground will be one with a good landing, — not a steep, muddy bank, — where there is plenty of wood, good water, and where the ground is dry and level. A small tree or two may have to be cut down, and all roots and "humps" should be removed. They make themselves very prominent before morning, even when covered generously with boughs.

The tent should be pitched with the head to windward, so that the smoke from the fire shall not be blown into it. It should also be well under shelter, in anticipation of high winds or heavy rain, and in a position where a heavy rain would not be likely to flood it.

The ridge-pole and uprights should be well trimmed of all projecting twigs which might make a hole in the tent, except that the uprights may have left on one side several such, on which to hang belts, cups, and the like. The uprights should be cut about nine feet long, with a slight notch on the upper end, and the lower end sharpened. Drive them into the ground, by their own weight, and work them from side to side, thus enlarging and deepening the holes until the poles are sunk sufficiently to stand out of ground the height of the tent. Then lay the latter out flat on its side, put the ridge-pole in its place, along the top of the tent, take down the uprights and insert them under the side of the tent, up against the ends of the ridge-pole, and, with one person holding each of the two poles, lift into a perpendicular position, and set them into their holes. They will usually stand alone while the pins (notched sticks) are being driven into the ground.

A string stretched across the tent, just under the ridge-pole, will make a good clothes-line for socks, towels, and the like. Guns and rods can be stacked around the pole at the head of the tent, at night, and made secure by a strap.

The historic camp-bed is made of fir-boughs, laid down in rows with the under side up, and overlapping each other shingle fashion, the larger part, or stem, being covered by the adjoining layer. It requires some knack to break off boughs from fir-trees. A quick snap, accomplished by the thumb and fore and middle fingers, does it.

Tables and seats can be improvised, and with a small amount of labor a camp can be considerably embellished. Two rubber blankets stretched over a ridge-pole, which is laid on, and tied to, the branches of adjoining trees, make an excellent canopy for the table. To provide a seat, select two trees about four or five feet apart; with your axe cut into them on the same side for several inches, about a foot and a half above ground. Then make several perpendicular cuts into this part of the trees, into which drive a wedge, which shall project about a foot, and a little above a horizontal. On these wedges lay poles cut the proper length, and you have your seat.

A candlestick may be made, by taking a stick as large round as your thumb, sharpening one end, splitting the other, and inserting the candle, which will be held in place by the elasticity of the wood. If not, it can be tied with a string or withe.

CAMP-FIRE.

The camp-fire should be built about six feet from the door of your tent. The large trunk of a tree, say five feet long and two feet in diameter, (or two smaller logs, one on top of the other,) makes your back-log, or reflector, while two smaller and shorter ones, placed at right angles to it, about four feet apart, make your "hand-junks," all of them preferably of hard wood. The active or burning part of the fire will be between the hand-junks, and it may readily be lighted with birch-bark. Dry soft-wood is usually abundant. Dead wood found lying on the ground is apt to be wet and soggy, and will not burn readily. Pull down two or three small dead trees, which can quickly be cut or broken up in lengths to suit. This serves well to kindle your fire, after which hard wood will be found hotter and less crackly.

The following woods are good for cooking, when dry, substantially in the order named: pine, fir, cedar, hemlock, and spruce. The last four kinds crackle considerably, and make a great quantity of ashes. A dead and partially decayed hemlock will burn well, and will not crackle very much.

All of the foregoing, when green, have a good deal of gum in them, except cedar, which splits easily, and is much used for tables, skin-stretchers, and the like.

Of the hard woods, rock-maple and yellow-birch are the hardest found in Northern Maine. The latter, being very tough, and usually growing to a much greater size than rock-maple, is good for back-logs and hand-junks, while white-birch is easily split, burns freely, but does not give as much heat as rock-maple or yellow-birch.

COOKING.

Having given the kinds of food suitable for camp, and the quantities of each to be provided, it may not be out of place to give a few hints as to its preparation for the table.

Fish chowder is one of the readiest of camp dishes, as well as one of the most palatable. Clean your fish, cut it into pieces about an inch long, peel and slice your potatoes, not too thin, and put into your pail alternate layers of fish and potatoes, together with a small quantity of pork or bacon cut into small squares, and a quarter of an onion chopped fine. Season each layer, as you put it in, with salt and pepper, and cover the whole with water. Boil about fifteen or twenty minutes, after which stir in one or two table-spoonfuls of condensed milk, add hard-bread, soaked or not, to suit the fancy, and leave on the fire a few moments longer. After the hard-bread shall have been added, great care should be taken that the mixture does not burn.

For duck, partridge, or musquash stew, cut the meat into small pieces, and place it in a pail, two thirds full of water, where it can boil gently. After half an hour or more, according to the tenderness of the meat, season to the taste, add two handfuls of pearled barley, and boil twenty minutes longer, taking care that the barley does not burn on the bottom of the pail. In the absence of barley, thicken with a little flour previously dissolved in cold water.

For white bread, a small quantity of baking powder, according to directions which accompany the latter, and a pinch of salt, should be thoroughly mixed with the flour, *dry*. Then add cold water, stir vigorously, and knead *ad libitum*. Bread can be baked in a regular baker, or in a frying-pan. The latter method requires good coals and a hot fire. Put the dough in the pan, which has been previously greased, and set the latter on a small bed of coals, a foot or more from the fire. Leave it there a few moments, until the under side shall have hardened enough to retain its shape. Then tilt the pan up, and support it by a crotched stick stuck into the hole in the end of the handle. The bed of coals behind and underneath, and the fire in front, will soon cook the loaf, which will need watching and turning.

"Flippers," or "flap-jacks," are mixed like bread, except that a little more baking powder is used, and a good deal more water.

Graham bread is made like wheat bread, except that a little sugar is added to the other ingredients. Any farinaceous article which contains sugar or molasses will, when baking, burn much more easily than one without sweets, and therefore needs more careful watching.

A good johnny-cake, or suet-cake, can be made of equal parts of wheat flour and corn meal. First mix in your baking powder, then cut up into small squares a piece of pork, try out the fat, and pour the whole into your pan with molasses and a little cold water. Stir briskly, and bake before a hot fire.

Some persons prefer "prepared" flour for camp use, but the writer has always had the best of success with baking powders.

For baked beans you need an iron pot with close-fitting cover, and a good dry bean-hole. The latter can be dug with the blade of your paddle, near the camp-fire. A fire should be made and kept ablaze in it for an hour or more, so as thoroughly to heat the ground. Pine bark, cherry, or black-birch sticks make good coals.

Pick over the beans, put them into a pail of water, and set on the fire after, or during, supper. Parboil until the skin can easily be rubbed off the beans, when the water must be drained off, and the beans transferred to their iron pot. Put a good piece of pork in the middle near the top, add two teaspoonfuls of molasses, and cover the whole with water. The coals should then be shovelled out of the hole, a few being left on the bottom, the covered pot set in and surrounded by coals, on top and on the sides. Cover the coals, in turn, with earth, and be careful not to leave any part uncovered, for the wind may fan the coals into too rapid combustion, and in the morning you will find your beans burnt.

It is hardly necessary to add directions for making tea and coffee, boiling or frying potatoes, or frying fish, except that fish should be put into the frying-pan only after the grease is thoroughly hot. Every one is supposed to know how these simpler dishes are prepared. Should any camper-out fail of the requisite knowledge, let him once become hungry, really "camp-hungry," and he will need no instructor. The art of cooking will come of itself.

DRESSING GAME.

The larger game of the woods is skinned by cutting through the hide, under the belly, from the tail to the neck, and laterally up the four legs and around the knees and hocks. The skin is then stripped or cut from the body, the animal lying on its back. The layer of flesh under the belly is deceptively thin. Therefore, in cutting through it to take out the entrails care must be exercised not to cut them. Their connection with the body is severed just back of the breast. The carcass should finally be washed thoroughly, and hung up by means of the sinews on the hind legs. All refuse matter should be buried at a long distance from camp.

The brisket, or breast, the "back-half," a part of the fore-quarter which runs on the ridge of the back on either side of the spine and above the ribs, and the hind-quarters, are generally the best parts of large game, while in the moose the tongue, nose, and lower lip, and in the beaver the tail and liver, are considered great delicacies.

The smaller fur-bearing animals, such as otter, mink, and musquash, are skinned by cutting across the end of the body from the hock of one leg to that of the other; then the lower parts of the hind-legs are cut off without being separated from the skin, which is pulled down, on all sides, over the body of the animal, after the manner of a stocking.

Trout are prepared for the frying-pan by being cut lengthwise along the belly, and having the entrails removed and the head and tail cut off. A pleasant flavor is imparted to them by hanging them where they will be in the smoke of the camp-fire for several hours.

HYGIENIC NOTES.

[The following pages are taken, with the kind permission of Dr. Elliott Coues, U. S. A., from that gentleman's valuable work on "Field Ornithology," (Salem, Naturalists' Agency,) and the advice given in them cannot fail to prove serviceable, both to those who go into the woods to camp out, and to those who stay at home. It is here offered again to the public by the writer of this little book, with a grateful sense of the obligation he, in common with many others, is under to its author.]

ACCIDENTS.

Always carry a loaded gun at half-cock, unless you are about to shoot. Unless the lock fail, accidental discharge is impossible, except under these circumstances: *a*, a direct blow on the nipple or pin; *b*, catching of both hammer and trigger simultaneously, drawing back of the former and its release whilst the trigger is still held, — the chances against which are simply incalculable. Full-cock, ticklish as it seems, is safer than no-cock, when a tap on the hammer or even the heel-plate, or a slight catch and release of the hammer, may cause discharge. Never let the muzzle of a loaded gun point toward your own person for a single instant. Get your gun over fences or into boats or carriages, before you get over or in yourself, or at any rate no later. Remove caps or cartridges on entering a house. Never aim a gun, loaded or not, at any object, unless you mean to press the trigger. Never put a loaded gun away long enough to forget whether it is loaded or not; never leave a loaded gun to be found by others under circumstances reasonably presupposing it to be unloaded. Never put a gun where it can be knocked down by a dog or a child. Never forget that, though a gunning accident may be sometimes interpretable (from a certain standpoint) as a "dispensation of Providence," such are dispensed oftenest to the careless. . . . .

The secret of safe *climbing* is never to relax one hold until another is secured; it is in spirit equally applicable to scrambling over rocks, a particularly difficult thing to do safely with a loaded gun. Test rotten, slippery, or otherwise suspicious holds, before trusting them. In lifting the body up anywhere keep the mouth shut, breathe through the nostrils, and go slowly.

In *swimming*, waste no strength unnecessarily in

trying to stem a current; yield partly, and land obliquely lower down; if exhausted, float, — the slightest motion of the hands will ordinarily keep the face above water; and in any event keep your wits collected. In fording deeply a heavy stone will strengthen your position. Never sail a boat experimentally; if you are no sailor, take one with you or stay on land.

In crossing a high, narrow footpath, never look lower than your feet; the muscles will work true, if not confused with faltering instructions from a giddy brain. On soft ground see what, if anything, has preceded you; large hoof-marks generally mean that the way is safe; if none are found, inquire for yourself before going on. Quicksand is the most treacherous, because far more dangerous than it looks; but I have seen a mule's ears finally disappear in genuine mud. Cattle-paths, however erratic, commonly prove the surest way out of a difficult place, whether of uncertain footing or dense undergrowth.

MIASM.

Unguarded exposure in malarious regions usually entails sickness, often preventable, however, by due precautions. It is worth knowing, in the first place, that miasmatic poison is most powerful between sunset and sunrise, — more exactly, from the damp of the evening until night vapors are dissipated; we may be out in the daytime with comparative impunity where to pass a night would be almost certain disease. If forced to camp out, seek the highest and driest spot, put a good fire on the swamp side, and also, if possible, let trees intervene. Never go out on an empty stomach; just a cup of coffee and a crust may make a decided difference. Meet the earliest unfavorable symptoms with quinine, — I should rather say, if unacclimated, anticipate them with this invaluable agent. Endeavor to maintain high health of all functions by the natural means of regularity and temperance in diet, exercise and repose.

"TAKING COLD."

This vague "household word" indicates one or more of a long varied train of unpleasant affections, nearly always traceable to one or the other of only two causes: *sudden change* of temperature, and *unequal distribution* of temperature. No extremes of heat or cold can alone effect this result; persons frozen to death do not "take cold" during the process. But if a part of the body be rapidly cooled, as by evaporation from a wet article of clothing, or by sitting in a draught of air, the rest of the body remaining at an ordinary temperature; or if the temperature of the whole be suddenly changed by going out into the cold, or, especially, by coming into a warm room, there is much liability of trouble. There is an old saying, "When the air comes through a hole, say your prayers to save your soul"; and I should think almost any one could get a "cold" with a spoonful of water on the wrist held to a key-hole. Singular as it may seem, sudden warming when cold is more dangerous than the reverse; every one has noticed how soon the handkerchief is required on entering a heated room on a

MT. KINEO—PEBBLE BEACH.

cold day. Frost-bite is an extreme illustration of this. As the Irishman said on picking himself up, it was not the fall, but stopping so quickly, that hurt him; it is not the lowering of the temperature to the freezing-point, but its subsequent elevation, that devitalizes the tissue. This is why rubbing with snow, or bathing in cold water, is required to restore safely a frozen part; the arrested circulation must be very gradually re-established, or inflammation, perhaps mortification, ensues. General precautions against taking cold are almost self-evident, in this light. There is ordinarily little if any danger to be apprehended from wet clothes, so long as exercise is kept up; for the "glow" about compensates for the extra cooling by evaporation. Nor is a complete drenching more likely to be injurious than wetting of one part. But never sit still wet; and in changing, rub the body dry. There is a general tendency, springing from fatigue, indolence, or indifference, to neglect damp feet; that is to say, to dry them by the fire; but this process is tedious and uncertain. I would say especially, off with the muddy boots and sodden socks at once, — dry stockings and slippers, after a hunt, may make just the difference of your being able to go out again or never.

Take care never to check perspiration; during this process the body is in a somewhat critical condition, and sudden arrest of the function may result disastrously, — even fatally. One part of the business of perspiration is to equalize bodily temperature, and it must not be interfered with. The secret of much that is to be said about *bathing* when heated, lies here. A person overheated, panting it may be, with throbbing temples and a *dry* skin, is in danger partly because the natural cooling by evaporation from the skin is denied, and this condition is sometimes not far from a "sunstroke." Under these circumstances, a person of fairly good constitution may plunge into the water with impunity, — even with benefit. But if the body be already cooling by sweating, rapid abstraction of heat from the surface may cause internal congestion, never unattended with danger. Drinking ice-water offers a somewhat parallel case; even on stooping to drink at the brook, when flushed with heat, it is well to bathe the face and hands first, and to taste the water before a full draught.

It is a well-known excellent rule, not to bathe immediately after a full meal; because during digestion the organs concerned are comparatively engorged, and any sudden disturbance of the circulation may be disastrous.

The imperative necessity of resisting drowsiness under extreme cold requires no comment.

In walking under a hot sun the head may be sensibly protected by green leaves or grass in the hat; they may be advantageously moistened, but not enough to drip about the ears. Under such circumstances the slightest giddiness, dimness of sight, or confusion of ideas, should be taken as a warning of possible sunstroke, instantly demanding rest, and shelter if practicable.

HUNGER AND FATIGUE

are more closely related than they might seem to be; one is a sign that the fuel is out, and the other asks for it. Extreme fatigue, indeed, destroys appetite; this simply means, temporary incapacity for digestion. But even far short of this, food is more easily digested, and better relished after a little preparation of the furnace. On coming home tired it is much better to make a leisurely and reasonably nice toilet than to eat at once, or to lie still thinking how tired you are; after a change and a wash you will feel like a "new man," and go to table in capital state. Whatever dietetic irregularities a high state of civilization may demand or render practicable, a normally healthy person is inconvenienced almost as soon as his regular meal-time passes without food; and few can work comfortably or profitably fasting over six or eight hours. Eat before starting; if for a day's tramp, take a lunch; the most frugal meal will appease if it do not satisfy hunger, and so postpone its urgency. As a small scrap of practical wisdom, I would add, keep the remnants of the lunch, if there are any; for you cannot always be sure of getting in to supper.

STIMULATION.

When cold, fatigued, depressed in mind, and on other occasions, you may feel inclined to resort to artificial stimulus. Respecting this many-sided theme I have a few words to offer of direct bearing on the [bird] collector's case. It should be clearly understood, in the first place, that a stimulant confers no strength whatever; it simply calls the powers that be into increased action at their own expense. Seeking real strength in stimulus is as wise as an attempt to lift yourself up by the boot-straps. You may gather yourself to leap the ditch and you clear it; but no such muscular energy can be sustained; exhaustion speedily renders further expenditure impossible. But now suppose a very powerful mental impression be made, say the circumstance of a succession of ditches in front, and a mad dog behind; if the stimulus of terror be sufficiently strong, you may leap on till you drop senseless. Alcoholic stimulus is a parallel case, and is not seldom pushed to the same extreme. Under its influence you never can tell when you *are* tired; the expenditure goes on, indeed, with unnatural rapidity, only it is not felt at the time; but the upshot is, you have all the original fatigue to endure and to recover from, *plus* the fatigue resulting from over-excitation of the system.

Taken as a fortification against cold, alcohol is as unsatisfactory as a remedy for fatigue. Insensibility to cold does not imply protection. The fact is, the exposure is greater than before; the circulation and respiration being hurried, the waste is greater, and as sound fuel cannot be immediately supplied, the temperature of the body is soon lowered. The transient warmth and glow over, the system has both cold *and* depression to endure; there is no use in borrowing from yourself and fancying you are richer.

Secondly, the value of any stimulus (except in a few exigencies of disease or injury) is in proportion, not to the intensity, but to the equableness and durability of its effect. This is one reason why tea, coffee, and articles of corresponding qualities, are preferable to alcoholic drinks; they work so smoothly that their effect is often unnoticed, and they "stay by" well;

the friction of alcohol is tremendous in comparison. A glass of grog may help a veteran over the fence, but no one, young or old, can shoot all day on whiskey....

Thirdly, undue excitation of any physical function is followed by corresponding depression, on the simple principle that action and reaction are equal: and the balance of health turns too easily to be wilfully disturbed. Stimulation is a draft upon vital capital, when interest alone should suffice; it may be needed at times to bridge a chasm, but habitual living beyond vital income infallibly entails bankruptcy in health. The use of alcohol in health seems practically restricted to purposes of sensuous gratification on the part of those prepared to pay a round price for this luxury. The three golden rules here are, never drink before breakfast, never drink alone, and never drink bad liquor; their observance may make even the abuse of alcohol tolerable. Serious objections for a naturalist, at least, are that science, viewed through a glass, seems distant and uncertain, while the joys of rum are immediate and unquestionable; and that intemperance, being an attempt to defy certain physical laws, is therefore eminently unscientific.

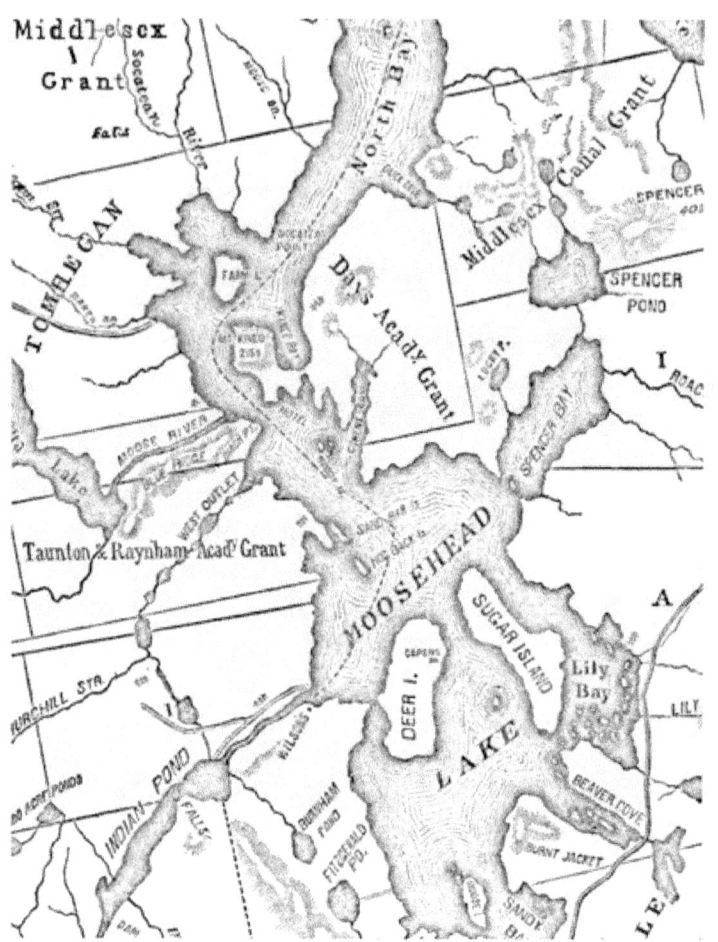

PART SECOND.

MOOSEHEAD LAKE AND IMMEDIATE VICINITY.

BOSTON TO BANGOR.

ONE can leave Boston, via the Eastern, or Boston and Maine, and Maine Central Railroads, at half past seven o'clock in the morning, arriving in Bangor the same evening, where a good night's rest may be enjoyed at any of the comfortable hotels of that city. The most expeditious way, and one perhaps as comfortable as any, is to leave Boston at seven o'clock in the evening, taking the Pullman train on the Eastern and Maine Central roads, and arrive in Bangor early the next morning, in time to eat a good breakfast at the well-kept restaurant in the depot, or at one of the hotels, before proceeding further. Luggage is checked through from Boston to Blanchard, the present terminus of the Bangor and Piscataquis Railroad.

The train of the European and North American Railway, which carries Moosehead Lake passengers from Bangor to Oldtown, is made up at the Maine Central depot, and leaves it some ten minutes before the time advertised for starting (7:30 A.M.). The depot of the European and North American Railway is a quarter of a mile beyond, on Exchange Street.

One can go by water from Boston to Bangor, leaving the former place at five o'clock, P.M., and reaching Bangor about noon the following day. By this route, however, one day and night are lost, as the afternoon train from Bangor to Blanchard is a mixed one, and arrives at Blanchard late at night. There are no night stages to Greenville, and no hotel accommodations at Blanchard station, except such as the restaurant offers.

BANGOR TO THE LAKE.

Leaving Bangor at half past seven in the morning, the train carries one along the west bank of the Penobscot, over the European and North American Railway, twelve miles, to Oldtown. Here from the car-window can soon be seen, across the water, the Indian island, with its church and numerous dwelling-houses, — an object of curiosity to all strangers.

At Oldtown the train divides, and an engine in waiting is attached to the Moosehead Lake cars, which it hurries over the Bangor and Piscataquis Railroad, as fast as prudence, and a regard for stray cows, will allow.

In clear weather good views of Mount Katahdin can be had from South Lagrange and from Milo.

The country through which the cars pass is pretty, although not specially interesting, until they near the town of Blanchard. Russell Mountain and other peaks then appear on the left, frowning down on the valley of the Piscataquis. The road-bed lies on the brow of a high ridge to the east of the valley, and affords many a picturesque view of the valley and mountains beyond.

The cars arrive at Blanchard station between eleven and half past eleven o'clock, and, after having had an opportunity to lunch in the restaurant at the depot, passengers mount the stage, and for five miles climb over a number of hills which lie between Blanchard and Shirley. At the latter place the horses are watered, fares collected, and with a merry crack of the whip the stage proceeds. The six miles of road between Shirley and Greenville are better than the other five, the hills shorter and less tedious, and, when within a mile or two of the lake, the scenery unfolds charmingly. Squaw Mountain looms up on the left, and the countless peaks of the Lily Bay and Ebeeme ranges stretch away to the east.*

GREENVILLE AND VICINITY.

Greenville, a small village with one church and about two hundred inhabitants, is at the southern end of Moosehead Lake, on an arm called the East Cove, and is the focus of the logging operations on the upper Kennebec and Penobscot waters. Supplies are hauled from here in winter over or around the lake to the various logging camps, and all travel to and from the camps is through Greenville.

* A telegraph line is being built from Dover to Greenville, and is expected to be completed during the present summer. The railroad bed is soon to be graded beyond its present terminus, and pushed through to the lake.

Apart from the arrival and departure of the stage there is nothing, in summer or winter, specially to interest strangers in Greenville, more than in many other favorite country resorts. The view of the lake from the village is pretty, although circumscribed, but perhaps the mountain-tops, and the snatches of water visible among the rocky and wooded islets near at hand, awaken a larger anticipation of the scenes and enjoyment still to come.

There are two hotels in Greenville, the Eveleth and Lake Houses, at either of which visitors are attentively cared for and hospitably entertained. Guests can obtain teams at reasonable rates, with or without a driver, to make excursions to Wilson Pond or elsewhere in the neighborhood. Campers-out will find several good stores at Greenville, where they can get almost all the necessary articles of camp fare, or of camp equipage, including canoes.

Near Greenville there are a number of ponds and streams in which trout abound, and which sportsmen frequently visit. The most noteworthy are the

WILSON PONDS,

the nearer of which is three miles distant, to the east. A good wagon-road runs two miles of the way, to a farm where teams can be left and baited. The other mile must be walked, and the path leads over the farm, down a steep bank to the lower and larger pond. Fish are taken here almost exclusively with bait, and it is said that when they bite here, they will not rise in the lake, and *vice versa*. Boats can be hired at fifty cents a day.

A boat-ride across the lower pond, and a short walk over a good path take one to the upper pond. One day is hardly enough to include a visit to this pond, if the excursionist expects to fish much.

Gerrish Pond lies west of Lower Wilson Pond, about two miles from Greenville, and also furnishes some bait-fishing.

Eagle Stream, two or three miles from the hotels, affords good fly-fishing.

From Greenville a variety of pretty trips may be made on the lake, by sail-boat or canoe, to occupy as much or as little time as one wishes, and one can spend a few days in this neighborhood very pleasantly and quietly.

FITZGERALD AND SQUAW PONDS.

From Greenville it is about seven miles by water to Johnson's Landing (a mile west of North Squaw Brook), whence a good road leads, half a mile, direct to Fitzgerald Pond. From this point the ascent is made of Squaw Mountain, one of the finest peaks, and perhaps the most prominent, around the lake. Squaw Pond can be reached from West Cove by a path two and a half miles long, or one can go the whole distance overland from Greenville, perhaps a mile further. A boat is usually kept at the pond. Squaw Brooks are not navigable by canoes. Fishing is sometimes good at their mouths, and in the ponds of which they are the outlets.

MOOSEHEAD LAKE.

Each renewed visit to Moosehead Lake attaches one more firmly to its magic presence and lovely views, every feature of which offers the returning traveller an indescribable welcome. Stretching here and there in irregular and broken confusion, its coves and bays grope about, as it were, like the arms of a cephalopod; studded with islands numerous as the days of the year, from the tiny rocklet with its scanty, half-starved offspring of bushes, to the more extended area, covered with prodigal growths of fir and spruce; surrounded by mountains whose soft outlines and ever-varying tints are objects of untiring admiration; — these and a thousand other beauties that steal unconsciously into the spirit, paint a wondrous picture, and fill one's being with fervent thanks to the Creator.

Moosehead Lake, nine hundred and sixty feet above sea-level, is about thirty-eight miles long, and varies in width from one to fourteen miles. Several hotels and taverns have sprung up, here and there, on its shores, and of late years the continuity of its dark green forests has been broken by the bright patches of farm lands, and white farm-houses peep up in many places, to indicate the thrift of their sturdy owners.

At Greenville will be found boats of all descriptions, from canoes to steamers. Tourists go up the lake either in sail-boats, which are to let by the day or week with the services of their owners, and as many more guides as may be necessary, or they take passage on one of the steamers which ply regularly between the foot of the lake and Kineo. They make two trips a day, in the season, between these places, and twice a week go beyond Kineo to the head of the lake. Their captains are very obliging, and to accommodate parties often go out of their regular course, to the East Outlet, Spencer Bay, and other points less distant. A steamer may at times be chartered for a day, or trip, at reasonable rates.

Soon after the arrival of the stage, the steamer leaves its wharf, and threads its way among a number of small islands past Burnt Jacket on the right, into an open expanse of water below Deer and Sugar Islands. Touching at Capen's Landing on Deer Island, half the journey (ten miles) is accomplished, and as the boat emerges from the narrow passage between the two islands, it enters the widest part of the lake. On the left, are the

EAST OUTLET, AND DAM,

where the Kennebec resumes its course, previously interrupted by the lake at the mouth of Moose River. A small hotel here accommodates a goodly number of guests, who frequent this favorite fishing-ground in September.

The Kennebec is very rapid immediately below the dam, and although a part of the distance between the dam and

INDIAN POND

is easy to run, it is considered safer to be hauled across, five miles, over a good road. On the right bank of the river about two miles below the dam is a farm, where a team can be secured, to do the necessary hauling. A road runs from the same farm to Churchill Stream. Indian Pond is divided into two parts, connected by a thoroughfare, and altogether is over three miles long. There is good fishing at the mouth of West Outlet Stream, in the thoroughfare, and at the outlet of the pond. Below this point the river is wild and "ragged" for seven miles, and canoes seldom venture to brave the perils of its navigation.

On the opposite side of the lake, Spencer Bay extends eastward four miles from narrows of the same name. Into its upper end empty Spencer Brook and Roach River. The latter stream flows some six or seven miles from

ROACH POND,

and is rapid, rocky, and hard to navigate. A road lies on the right bank. The better way to reach the pond is by road from Greenville. A tavern stands on the shore of Lily Bay, near the mouth of North Brook. From here to Roach Pond is seven miles, and to Greenville, thirteen. A team can be procured at the Lily Bay House to haul one to Davis's, at the outlet of Roach Pond, where there is a substantial hotel and all the comforts which care and attention can provide in this isolated region. At the dam in the river, near the hotel, and in pools below the dam, and also at the upper end of the pond, good trout-fishing is to be had. On the north of the brook at this end of the pond is a small log-camp. From the mouth of the same brook, on the south side, a good logging road leads a mile and a half or more, southeast, to Little Pleasant Pond, where there is good fishing. A half-mile or more beyond is a larger pond, where the trout are larger.

Between the First and Second Roach Ponds the stream is not very rapid, but full of gravel-beds, and apt, in summer, to be very shallow. On the south shore of the Second Pond, on the road from Katahdin Iron-Works to Chesuncook Lake, is a farm where one can get a meal, and, if needed, a supply of flour and pork.

SPENCER POND

empties through Spencer Brook, two miles, into the bay of the same name. In low water a canoe will have to be dragged up the brook, or carried over a good road, which lies to the west of it. At the western end of the pond, which is about a mile and a half in diameter and substantially round, is a bog where cranberries grow in profusion. The usual camping-ground is on the northeast side of the pond, diagonally across from the outlet, and about midway between the fishing grounds, — two small streams which come into the pond, one on the north, and the other at the southeast corner. The north brook is sometimes hard to find. Its outlet is concealed by several small grassy islands. A mile up the brook is Little Spencer Pond. Spencer Mountains lie to the east of the pond; the nearer rises perhaps half a mile from its shore. They are both very steep, and hard to climb. Into Spencer Bay, on the west, empties a brook which comes from

LUCKY POND.

This little sheet of water is rather narrow, and about three quarters of a mile long. It is a boggy place, and good ground for deer and caribou. A canoe can run up the brook some distance in dead water, and one then steps out into the road which runs up the right side of the stream to the dam, where it crosses and goes around the pond. It is only about fifty rods from the head of the " dead " water to the pond, and little more than a mile from the latter to the lake.

Until the steamer leaves Deer Island, Mount Kineo has been hidden from sight. Little Kineo, however, to the east of it, resembles it so much, in the distance, as to be mistaken for it. Six miles from Capen's the steamer passes Hog Back and Sand Bar Islands on the left, and as it approaches its goal the indistinct cluster of white buildings at the foot of Mount Kineo is more easily separated into its component parts. Two miles from Sand Bar, Moody Islands are passed, on the right, and after two miles more the boat steams into the cove just east of the hotel, and is soon moored to its wharf.

MOUNT KINEO,

one of the largest hornstone mountains in the world, is midway up the lake, and, connected with its eastern shore by a narrow neck of land, forms quite a promontory. A sheer precipice on the south and east sides, it falls away less abruptly towards the west, and

MT. KINEO — TABLE ROCK.

slopes gradually to the north, affording at its base very good farming land. On this slope, at Hard-Scrabble, is raised, each year, a considerable quantity of grain and hay, on which the Kineo House stock is fed.

The eastern cliff of the mountain hangs over Kineo Bay. Its perpendicular height above the water is over eight hundred feet, and the lake at its base is, in one place, more than eight hundred feet deep.

From the cliff, skirting around northeast, runs a very pretty beach, divided, by a stretch of rocky, wooded shore, into two parts, — Cliff Beach, less than a mile from the hotel, and Pebble Beach, a mile and a half from it. From Table Rock off Cliff Beach, a few yards from shore, good fishing may be had late in the season. In fact, good fishing may be had, from canoes, all around Kineo Bay, and all the way around the mountain.

The south cliff is inaccessible except in one place near the western end, up a rift in the rock, where by the aid of trees men can find foothold for a very steep climb. The descent of the mountain by this route, to the hotel, can be made in half an hour.

The usual ascent is made from the southwest corner of the mountain, — Kineo Point, — and necessitates a boat-ride of about a mile from the "Three Sisters," — a group of pine-trees on the beach west of the hotel. Two and a half or three hours are enough to accomplish the round trip comfortably, and the view one gets from the summit well repays the toil of climbing. A cool spring on the top furnishes refreshing drink to the thirsty.

From a point on the water, between Kineo Point

and the Three Sisters, or perhaps a little further from shore than on the direct line between them, may be seen a good profile, on the southeast corner of the mountain.

LEGEND.

Moosehead Lake, like many other places, has its Indian legends, and has been the scene of many a bloody encounter between dusky tribes of the past. At the narrows between Sugar Island and the mainland, parts of the St. John (?) and Penobscot tribes are said to have met in a battle, in which the former were almost annihilated.

The legend of Kinneho, the gloomy chief, and of his squaw-mother, Maquaso, each of whom has given name to one of the principal mountains near Moosehead Lake, is not without pathetic interest. Kinneho, as a boy, grew up with more than usual Indian taciturnity, and with ever-increasing gloominess of disposition. His mother watched the development of these characteristics with anxiety and disappointment. He gave little heed to her solicitude, neglected and avoided her, and even shunned the companionship of the members of his tribe.

One morning Maquaso disappeared. Suspicion of foul play at once fell on the undutiful son. Kinneho, although a brave warrior, was henceforth excluded from the councils of his tribe. He went forth, and for a long time was seen no more. One day, however, he suddenly reappeared in the midst of a severe fight, in which his old companions were being worsted. His efforts turned defeat into victory, and he disappeared again, as mysteriously as he had come. Months went by. A solitary fire shone out, night after night, on the top of a mountain near the village of Kinneho's tribe, whose sides were all but inaccessible. No one dared approach the frowning rock, nor brave the anger of its dread inhabitant.

The exile lived on alone, in remorse lest he had been the cause of his unhappy mother's disappearance. Night after night he kept vigil, his uneasy glance scanning the horizon, as if impelled by an unseen power. One night, afar off to the south, against the side of a mountain twenty miles away, he spied a twinkling light. The thought seized him that his mother must be there. Through the forest he made his way towards it. The next night the fire shone out again through the trees. He neared it, and there before him stood his long-lost mother. Leaping to her side, he grasped her aged form in his strong arms, only to see the gleam of recognition in her eyes, and to hear her dying sob, as the broken spirit passed away, peaceful at last.

THE MT. KINEO HOUSE

is on flat ground south of the mountain, and with its stables and dependencies, all painted white, stands out in marked contrast to the wildness of the surrounding scenes. Its spacious walls are capable of accommodating four hundred people, and in the season the house and grounds are alive with pleasure-seekers from the busy world without.

Walking, boating, canoeing, bowling, croquet, and

billiards are the principal pastimes of its guests. Besides the walks to Cliff and Pebble Beaches, which lead partly through pasture lands and partly through woods, and the climb up the mountain, there is little walking to be done.

The Mystic Grotto, a mile and a half from the hotel, where a cliff thirty feet high hangs over a shady spot in the woods; the gold mine, a mile and a quarter from the hotel; and the Devil's Delight, at the foot of the cliff, are all near Cliff and Pebble Beaches, and serve to give a slight variety to one's ramblings.

About a mile and a quarter from the Three Sisters, southwest, and off Birch Point, is a buoy, kept well baited in summer, where white-fish and "lakers" of considerable size are often caught. In nearly the same direction, a little more westerly, and a mile and a half from the Three Sisters, is the mouth of Moose River, properly the Kennebec. Up the river for a mile and a half the water is "dead," and offers a pretty morning or afternoon excursion.

The paddle or sail around the mountain — six miles — is somewhat more of an undertaking, but enjoyable. A small boat is usually to be found on Cliff Beach, which parties who walk over the neck can use, to row under the cliff, — perhaps a good substitute for a paddle around the mountain.

In the other direction, east, one can paddle a quarter of a mile to Little Gull Rock, a mile and a quarter to Big Gull Rock, and two miles and a half to Cowen's Cove. The latter is principally noted for the abundance of frogs which live in the grassy land at its head. In the same direction, on the shore beyond Little Gull

Rock is a miniature pond, separated from the lake by a strip of land a few feet wide, and at its upper end is a cranberry bog. This is the narrowest part of the neck.

Moody Islands, two miles south of the hotel, furnish at times good deep-water fishing.

Guests of the Mount Kineo House, who go into camp for a few days, can have their rooms locked up during their absence, and are provided with provisions for the excursion. These include all the usual articles of camp-fare, such as pork, potatoes, flour, baking powder, hard bread, butter, sugar, coffee, tea, salt, pepper, and the like, but no canned goods. No reduction is made on the bills of persons who go in this way. The alternative is to give up one's room, buy one's provisions, and trust to good fortune to secure a room on one's return.

Connected with the hotel at Kineo is a store, where all staple articles of food, and some luxuries, can be bought. The prices asked are just enough above retail prices at Greenville, or anywhere else, to cover the extra cost of transportation, and to leave a small margin for profit.

Fishing tackle of good quality can be bought or hired of the superintendent of the hotel.

It is to be hoped that the conservative spirit dominant thus far at Kineo, among its *habitués*, will still continue to shape its customs of plain dress and reasonable hours of rising and retiring. Gentlemen can live in woollen shirts, and appear in them at all times, without giving offence or appearing discourteous, while ladies are not obliged to make a change of toilet for each meal. Saratoga trunks and elegant dresses are deservedly frowned down, and are utterly out of place. Man comes here to renew his vital energy; and his every impulse — let it be said to his credit — is to throw aside the questionable requirements of fashion, which in most summer resorts hamper his freedom, and tend to sap his vitality instead of quickening it.

Besides the short excursions by water, already noted, one can paddle — or ride in the "Day Dream," a tiny steamer belonging to the Kineo House — about three miles south of the hotel, to the

WEST OUTLET.

Much less water passes out of the lake here than at the other outlet, and consequently the stream, which runs nine miles to Indian Pond, is rapid, shallow, and rocky, except where broken by ponds. Of these there are eight or nine. The first lies within twenty-five rods of the lake, and is hardly more than a "logon." A like distance beyond the first is the second pond, which is a mile long and half as wide. The third is a small round pond, or perhaps more properly only a stretch of "dead" water in the stream. Beyond it, half a mile from number two, is number four, twenty-five rods wide and half a mile long. Twenty rods more bring one into number five, which is half a mile long and nearly as wide. The sixth lies twenty rods beyond, is round and deep, and has a rocky shore. The seventh is three quarters of a mile from number six, and is a mile long and about half as wide. At its foot used to be a dam, at Bodfish Falls. Canoes can be "dropped" over the ledges here, which together are about six feet high. The mouth of Churchill Stream is just below the falls, and one must paddle up it a mile and a half to the dam, where the best fishing is to be found.

A mile below Churchill Stream is a stretch of "dead" water, by some called the "Alder Ground," and by others Long Pond. It is a mile and a half long, and perhaps thirty rods wide. A short distance below it is Round Pond, the last of the series, and one of the largest, above which, on the left, at the mouth of a small brook, trout are to be found. It is a mile and a half or more from Round Pond into Indian Pond.

BRASSUA LAKE

lies to the west of Moosehead, and its lower end is due west of Kineo. One goes up Moose River for a mile and a half, through "dead" water, to a small island, opposite which non-working members of a party take to the path on the north side, while the canoes push up the stream two and a half miles, through rapid water, to the lake. The worst places are the dam, and Sam's Pitch, a few rods above it. At the former it is well for the inexperienced canoe-man to get out and draw his boat up by the "painter"; at the latter promptness of action only is needed.

Brassua Lake is six or seven miles long, and from one to two wide. At its southwest corner, opposite the outlet, is the mouth of Miseree Stream, once, and even now, a good fishing-ground. It is navigable for only a short distance. The favorite camp-grounds have always been on the south shore of the Lake. Into its northeastern end empties

BRASSUA STREAM,

quite a pretty little river, and which, with the exception of a short stretch of rapids two miles from the mouth, is navigable for three or four miles. In a little pond above the rapids, and in the stream beyond, are good feeding-grounds for ducks. Just below the rapids are good trout-holes and fair camping sites.

Midway up the lake, and flowing into it from the west, is

MOOSE RIVER

again. About two miles of smooth, deep water bring one to the mouth of Tom Fletcher Brook, a good fishing-ground, named after a trapper who was drowned in the rapids up the river. Report says he was trapping in the woods with two companions, and, at the close of the season, returned alone to camp one day, took all the fur, and hurried down stream with it. The judgment of Heaven seems to have overtaken him, for his body was soon found some miles below camp, and was buried at the mouth of the brook.

A short distance above this spot the river widens and forms Little Brassua Pond. Here are a number of grass-islands, which afford play-ground to muskrats and hiding-places to ducks.

From this point up, the river is rapid, and it requires a good deal of energy to stem its current with a loaded canoe. The Rolling Dam Ledge, a mile and a quarter above Little Brassua, and just below Coburn's Farm, is an obstacle over which a canoe will have to be lifted.

Three miles more of strong, and in some places rapid water, intervene before the dam is reached. Above it, for two miles and a quarter or more, the current is strong, but navigation is good. Stony Brook Rapids are about one hundred rods long. At the dam, and at the mouths of the several brooks which flow into Long Pond, good fishing may be had.

LONG POND

is some ten miles long, and of irregular shape. Its shores are attractive to the camper-out, and afford some very pleasing glimpses of landscape, with mountains in the background. Seven miles of a winding and substantially smooth water-course lie between Long Pond and Wood Pond, although it is only four miles by land from one to the other. Moose River Bridge is half a mile below the latter pond, and over it passes the Canada Road.*

TOMHEGAN RIVER

empties into a cove about six miles from Kineo, on the west side of Moosehead Lake. It is an interesting stream, and well repays a visit. About two miles from the mouth, or perhaps less, are some "rips," above which "dead" water reappears for a time, and open

---

* The description of Moose River above Wood Pond will be found in another place.

alder-land soon takes the place of dark, overhanging banks. A canoe will have to be carried around these "rips." Fishing can be had at the mouth, and in pools near it. From the "rips" a good road runs, some seven miles, up the left bank of the stream to the pond, around whose shores great quantities of cranberries grow.

Four miles from Tomhegan, and about seven northwest from Kineo, in an extensive bay, is the mouth of

SOCATEAN RIVER,

one of the prettiest streams that empty into the lake. Its water near the mouth is without perceptible current, black, and apparently deep, and its banks are sprinkled with graceful hackmatacks, and fringed with bright-hued grass, mingling, at the water's edge, with lily-pads.

Four miles up the stream are the Falls and Pool, formerly a favorite resort for camping parties, but not so popular since the ravaging fire which ran through the forest there several years ago. Fishing is good at the mouth, and here and there up the stream, especially above the Pool and at the upper Falls, which are three miles from it. A good road runs up the east side of the stream.

DUCK COVE,

on the east shore of the lake, midway between Kineo and the Northeast Carry, and about ten miles from the former, lies under the shadow of a small mountain.

Back of it, and on an open road half a mile long, is a pond, where of late years fishing has been good. The road begins on the south side of the brook.

Baker Brook, in a deep cove just above the mouth of Moose River; Moose Brook, above Socatean Point, and Williams Stream, opposite Centre Island, — all of them on the west side of the lake, — afford more or less fishing, but the "catch" is apt to be small in size, if not in numbers.

The lake, after growing wider near Kineo, narrows again at Socatean Point, between which and Farm Island is a stretch of water known as the Devil's Blowhole. The wind is ever contrary here, causing "chop-waves" in profusion, and is consequently annoying to canoe-men.

Beyond Socatean Point is one unbroken expanse of water, almost as far as the eye can reach, the land at the head of the lake being so low as to be scarcely distinguishable.

Shaw's farm-house, opposite Socatean Point, is the only habitation on the lake above Kineo, until one reaches the Northeast and Northwest Carries.

SOCATEAN FALLS AND POOL.

TOURS BEYOND MOOSEHEAD LAKE.

PENOBSCOT WATERS.

NORTHEAST CARRY.

A SMALL hotel stands on the shore of Moosehead Lake, at the end of the Northeast Carry, and affords comfortable accommodation and good fare to a limited number of guests. The steamer lands its passengers here twice a week, on Tuesdays and Fridays, and they dine at the hotel.

Tourists can have their canoes and luggage hauled over the carry, two miles, to the Penobscot, for a dollar and a half each. There are two teams to be had, one at the hotel, and the other from Joe Morris's farm, at the other end of the carry. Each team can take two canoes and their luggage at a load. The road rises gradually towards the middle from each end, and is pretty level, but wet and muddy after a rain.

Blueberries grow in profusion in this neighborhood, and the remains are still visible of an old tram-way over which formerly lumbermen's supplies were hauled to the Penobscot.

WEST BRANCH OF THE PENOBSCOT, GOING DOWN FROM NORTHEAST CARRY.

Leaving Morris's, where the river is deep and sluggish, a two-mile paddle through "dead" water brings one to the mouth of Lobster Stream. Below here there is a strong current with some "rips" for two miles and a half more, when a small island is reached, where the water again becomes "dead." Three and a half miles more of unvaried still water bring one to Moosehorn Stream, a small tributary on the right. From this point to the head of Pine Stream Falls (seven miles), there is very little still water, the distance to Chesuncook Lake being made up of the following stretches, viz. : —

Moosehorn to Sears's Clearing (on the right)	2m.
Sears's to Ragmuff Stream (on the left) . .	¼m.
Ragmuff to head of Big Island	1¼m.
Big Island to Fox Hole	+½m.
Fox Hole to head of Rocky Rips	2½m.
Head of Rocky Rips to foot of Pine Stream Falls	1½m.
Foot of Pine Stream Falls to Chesuncook Lake	2m.

Go to the right of Big Island, at the head of which, for a few rods, the river is rather shallow, but, except in dry seasons, there is depth enough to carry at least a canoe and luggage safely through to Fox Hole. Here the channel turns sharply to the left, lying within two feet, or less, of the left bank, and soon deepens again.

All the way from Morris's to Chesuncook Lake there runs along the right bank of the river a good road, which will be found very convenient to those who have to walk past shallow parts of the stream.

From the head to the foot of Rocky Rips is, perhaps, half a mile. Looking back from below them, when the river is at its ordinary summer height, no water can be seen in it at all, so thickly is its bed sprinkled with rocks and boulders.

A short stretch of dead water, containing several small grass-islands, separates Rocky Rips from Pine Stream Falls, the worst place in this part of the river. There are three principal "pitches," or falls, followed by perhaps three quarters of a mile of strong rapids. The writer's experience has been that it is better to go over the first pitch in the middle of the stream, then to the left over both the second and third pitches, but the height of the water at different times may make it expedient to change this course. In very high water, an easy passage by all three pitches may be found close to the left bank.

Rounding a bend about a mile below the rapids, one comes upon a huge pier in the river, and at about the same time bursts upon one's sight the glorious Katahdin group of mountains, twenty miles to the east.

Fair camping-grounds may be found here and there along the river, a convenient one being just above Pine Stream Falls on the left bank, nearly opposite the mouth of Pine Stream.

Of all the tributaries of the West Branch, passed in these eighteen miles, Lobster Stream is the only one navigable for any considerable distance, the water in it being deep enough to admit of easy passage to Lobster Lake, two miles away, even in times of drouth.

There is little fishing to be had on this route, except at Fox Hole, in a small inlet on the left, where there are supposed to be cold springs, and on the right and left among some small grass-islands below Pine Stream Falls, where there is quite a gravel-bar in the river.

It takes, ordinarily, a little more than two hours to go from Morris's to Moosehorn, and from there to Chesuncook Lake from four to five hours more.

LOBSTER LAKE

is so called from the little fresh-water lobsters, or crawfish, with which its waters abound. So level is its outflowing stream, that, after a heavy rain and rise of the West Branch, the former flows back. The lake is elbow-shaped, and its northern shore is marshy, while that of the lower arm is bolder, and rocky formation predominates. Several cold streams flow into it from the south, and pleasing camp-grounds offer themselves on the west. Few fish are to be found there. Fine views of Spencer Mountains and Mount Katahdin can be had from the middle of the lake.

A trip of three or four days, to this place, makes a pleasant excursion from Kineo.

CHESUNCOOK LAKE,

a "bulge" in the Penobscot, as it has been properly called, is eighteen miles long, and from one to three miles wide. It is without special attraction, save the glorious view it offers of old Katahdin, and, when head-winds are blowing over its surface, becomes quite

CHESUNCOOK LAKE.

an obstacle to rapid, or even moderate progress, on the part of the canoe-man.

From five to six hours are usually consumed in paddling over this lake, which time is increased or diminished according to the direction of the prevailing wind.

A temporary camping-ground may be found near Weymouth Point, or opposite and a little above it, on a small sandy point, near which is a cold brook. Meals and lodging are provided at Murphy's (now Hatheway's), at the head of the lake.

Among other streams flowing into Chesuncook Lake, and not elsewhere described, are Moose Brook and Caribou Stream.

MOOSE BROOK

flows from a pond of the same name about a mile from the lake. Its water is dead, and a canoe can be taken up through it into Moose Pond, and from there through more or less quick water to Cuxabexis Lake. Between Moose and Duck Ponds it is somewhat harder for a canoe to go. There is a dam at the outlet of Cuxabexis Lake, and good camping-ground may be found near its western end, towards the south. This group of ponds is seldom visited by sportsmen, and little is known of their attractions in the way of fish and game.

CARIBOU LAKE

lies to the southwest of Chesuncook Lake, and is connected with it by a "dead" stream about two miles long, which in some places is broad and covered with lily-pads, and makes a good feeding-ground for ducks. The lake is seven miles long. Its shores offer few inducements to campers. Several streams empty into it, in which there is some fishing to be had early in the autumn.

RIPOGENUS LAKE.

At the lower end of Chesuncook Lake the river narrows again for half a mile, flows over a succession of falls, and again widens into Ripogenus Lake. At Chesuncook dam, and in pools below it, good trout are often taken, and occasionally a salmon.

The carry lies several rods south of the dam, and is a good solid road. Canoes may be put into the stream at the end of half a mile, but the most of one's load will have to be carried a quarter-mile further to the shore of the lake, in order to avoid the dangers of the intervening rapids. From and at the head of Ripogenus Lake begins a series of views of Mount Katahdin and the Sourdnahunk range, which fairly enchant the lover of nature. Ever shifting as one moves on, now hidden by forest or intervening ridge, now bursting suddenly forth again in greater majesty, old Katahdin's silent and more vivid presence excites our awe and commands our admiration.

Ripogenus Lake is two miles long and a mile or more broad. It is a favorite camp-ground for tourists going down the river, and, aside from the picturesqueness of its situation, has quite an attraction in the wildness of the river at its foot.

Good fishing may be had off the mouth of Frost

Brook, and in pools below the lake. There is a cold spring in a cove on the south shore near the outlet.

HARRINGTON LAKE.

Into the northwest corner of Ripogenus Lake flows a stream of the same name, whose bed in summer ordinarily contains too little water for successful navigation. At high water, however, a canoe can be poled and led over rapids for four miles to the dam. Island Falls, a pitch four feet high, is about midway between Ripogenus Lake and the dam. Above the dam there is dead water for nearly two miles, then half a mile of quick water, followed by a small pond, and a rocky but smooth stretch of water which opens into Harrington Lake. A good path runs on the right side of the stream up to the dam, where it meets the road from Chesuncook Lake and continues on the same side up Harrington Stream almost to the lake, crossing between the latter and the small pond already mentioned. From this point it follows Soper, or Wadleigh, Brook on the west for two miles, crosses at a dam, and runs up the east side, along a three-mile bog, nearly to the source of the stream. It runs within two miles of Sourdnahunk Lake.

Harrington Lake is about three miles long and one mile wide, and lies prettily surrounded by hard-wood ridges, which afford many good camping-grounds. On the southwest shore, about two thirds of the way up the lake, and over a ridge, is a small pond where trout are said to abound.

Flowing into the lake at its head is a small stream,

which connects it with two small ponds a mile or less apart, the second pond being half a mile from Slaughter Pond, whose waters flow into the West Branch through Sourdnahunk Stream. Harrington Lake is reached, perhaps most easily, from Chesuncook Lake, by the road above mentioned.

FROST POND

lies about two miles north of Ripogenus Lake. A fair road leads to it from near the mouth of its outflowing brook, and to the east of it. The pond contains plenty of small trout, but without a canoe or raft it is hard to get at them, so densely wooded are the shores, to the very water's edge. The top of Katahdin is visible from the west shore of the pond.

WEST BRANCH OF THE PENOBSCOT, BELOW RIPOGENUS LAKE.

The outlet of Ripogenus Lake is ordinarily a narrow and deep gorge, where the water foams and hisses in its rapid course between walls of rock. After freshets, the river flows over a broader channel to the right, or south, of the entrance to the gorge, leaving quite a high and wooded island between the two. From this point, for a mile and a half, a good path runs along the river-bank, and enables one to get a fine view of perhaps the most wonderful, if not the most interesting, part of the Penobscot. Nearly the entire distance is a gorge with steep cliffs on either side, over a hundred feet high, in some places overhanging the stream, and with isolated masses of precipitous rock between them, whose tops

RIPOGENUS GORGE — LOOKING EAST.

are level with the banks on either side, and covered, like them, with ferns and blueberry-bushes. The water seems to have worn away the rock and soil around these islands, giving them the shape of an old-fashioned flat-iron, whence they derive the names of Big and Little Heater. The river pitches through this gorge in a succession of rapids, — none very high, but together making a fall of two hundred feet or more.

The carry from Ripogenus begins at the lower end of the lake, to the right of the outlet. At the end of a mile one descends a short hill, and on the right can be seen from the road

CARRY POND,

which used to be famous for its trout. In the absence of canoes a raft formerly served indifferently to bear people across the pond to the spring-hole where the fish lay. This pond has been so thoroughly fished of late years, that its supplies may not now always prove equal to the demand made upon them.

Half a mile from Carry Pond, on the road, is a large boulder on the brow of a steep descent. It lies in the middle of a small clearing, and from its top one gets a wide prospect over the valley below, and a fine view of Katahdin.

At the foot of this steep descent, and beyond a small brook, a path turns off to the left and leads to the "putting-in place," below which is a cold spring. Half a mile further brings one to an old river-drivers' camp, from which another path leads down the bank to the "Arches," — another difficult and dangerous impediment in the river. From here it is a mile to the end of the carry.

Canoes may take to the water again at the "putting-in place," but the stream below is dangerous, and there are three places where one has to lift over. Around one of them, the Arches, one must carry for thirty or forty rods on either bank. It is safer and more expeditious to carry over the whole three miles of road, than to attempt to run the river below the "putting-in place." A brook, the outlet of Carry Pond, empties into the river at the last-named point; the path to the latter crosses it twice after leaving the main road.

Once fairly embarked below the carry, one glides easily down stream through rapid water, lifting over one rocky pitch, and at the end of two and a half miles or more reaches Gulliver Pitch or Ambajemackomus Carry. This carry is about one hundred rods long, and begins at the foot of a steep descent in the river-bed, in a very rocky bend on the right.

Below Gulliver Pitch begins the dread "horse-race," which extends for nearly two miles, to within half a mile of dead water. The river is impetuous, and its bed ledgy, — refusing setting-pole hold. On all sides are dangerous rocks to be avoided, which call forth the canoe-man's skill, and put his nerve to the test. With care, however, one can run these rapids in safety, and will soon find himself in

SOURDNAHUNK DEAD-WATER,

one of the most attractive camping-grounds on the route. The river widens out considerably, and par-

RIPOGENUS GORGE — LOOKING WEST.

takes of the character of a miniature lake, with a grassy "logon" on the right. It is a mile and a half to its lower end, where one gets a very fine view of Katahdin to the east, and a pretty but less pretentious picture to the west.

A good path follows the river on the right bank, as far as the dead water. There is a good spring on the same side, at the foot of the "horse-race."

Leaving Sourdnahunk (sometimes pronounced Sowadehunk) Dead-Water, a short run brings one to the carry of the same name, on the left. Care should be taken not to overlook and run past it, as the stream immediately beyond looks smooth, and a canoe once in the current might easily be swept along and over the falls (five feet), with serious consequences. Just below the carry, which is less than thirty rods long, and on the same side, is a good spring. Half a mile below the falls is the mouth of Sourdnahunk Stream, below which for two miles one finds good canoeing, mostly through "dead" water, to the mouths of Aboljackomegus and Sandy Streams. At this point parties usually camp who intend to make the

ASCENT OF MOUNT KATAHDIN.

From a short distance up Sandy Stream — the more easterly brook — the path runs four or five miles over intervening ridges to the base of the mountain; the ascent thence continues up the slide on the southwest side of the mountain. It is perhaps less fatiguing to leave one's camp on the river bank early in the afternoon, with blankets, axe, and enough food for two days, — as light a load as possible, — and camp that night at the foot of the slide, or at the brook about a mile from it. With an early start the next morning, one can in three hours climb (at an angle of about sixty degrees) to the broad table-land, near the top of the mountain.

Here will be found, under and at the sides of several large rocks, springs or pools of water, cool, but of indifferent taste. There is said to be another and better spring part way up the slide, and to the east of it. As one ascends the mountain, vegetation becomes stunted, and disappears almost altogether just before the table-land is reached. A thick bed of dry moss covers the table-land, and a few dead and snarly roots scattered over it furnish scanty fuel to those who wish to make a cup of tea, or to warm themselves. The summit of the mountain is about a mile east of the springs, and the ascent to it is gradual and easy. A flat surface of not more than twenty feet in diameter forms the western peak. To the west of it lies the table-land. On the east, perhaps a quarter of a mile, is another peak, said to be ten feet lower than the first. Between the two is a ridge so narrow, that *one step* towards the north would send one into eternity over a sheer precipice hundreds of feet high. On the south side, the mountain, although not so precipitous, is exceedingly steep, and a misstep might result in as certain, though not so quick, a death. When the wind blows with any considerable force, one can cross from peak to peak only by creeping. From the eastern peak a spur of the mountain runs northeast for some distance, and has apparently the same general characteristics as the ridge just described. Surrounded by these walls and by Wassataquoik or Pomolah Mountain on the northwest, is a deep basin containing several ponds, one of which with no visible outlet is said to be so deep as never to have been fathomed by any ordinary sounding-line.

On a clear day, it is said, one can see from the top of Katahdin five hundred distinct and separate pieces of water. Millinokett Lake and Katahdin Pond are perhaps the prettiest bodies of water near at hand.

They who go up the mountain should be provided with extra warm clothing, as the change of temperature from below is apt to be very marked, and sometimes severe. At other times, however, the sun seems hotter on top than at the bottom of the mountain, but this is very exceptional. Ladies have climbed Katahdin, but only the strongest can do it.

From the summit to the foot of the slide one can descend in an hour and a half, and from the latter point to the river in two hours and a half more.

There is fishing at the mouth of Sandy Stream, — for eels as well as for trout.

Half a mile below Abol. Stream one comes to Abol. Falls, and a mile beyond to Pockwockamus Falls. At each place the carry is on the right, and less than half a mile long. Pockwockamus Dead-Water, above the falls of the same name, is narrow and crooked, and contains two or three islands. From it, as well as from various other points on the river below it, good views are obtained of Katahdin, which slowly recedes, and whose outlines gradually grow more dim. Below Pockwockamus Falls is Katepskonegan, or Debsconeak Dead-Water. It extends about three miles, to falls of the same name, around which through the woods, on the right, is a good carry, three quarters of a mile long.

The river is substantially "dead" below these falls, for four miles, and in one place is almost a mile wide, and has several islands in it.

Passamagamock Falls, at the foot of the dead water, may be run on the setting-pole, or the carry on the left can be used. Above and below them ponds empty into the river through streams navigable by canoes. Two miles intervene between Passamagamock Falls and Ambajejus Falls, which can also be run, at low water. In high water, however, it is dangerous for heavy-laden canoes to attempt passage. The carry lies on the left, and is about half a mile long. Below the falls, a half a mile, the river opens out into Ambajejus Lake, a pretty sheet of water some four miles long. It is in two parts, connected by a thoroughfare, the lower part being much the larger.

A narrow passage divides Ambajejus Lake from Pamedomcook Lake, quite a large body of water, only one end of which is crossed in going down the river.

Two miles or more lead one into another passage between Pamedomcook and North Twin Lakes. The shores here are so cut up into bays and coves, reaching here and there in confusion, that it is hard to tell when one is going amiss.

Four miles through North Twin Lake, and two miles down the river, bring one to the dam, where at a house on the bank one can obtain a good meal.

From the North Twin dam passing through Quakish

Lake one mile, and through a mile of rapid water below it, one comes to Fowler's Carry. This is two miles long, and at the other end of it a team can be obtained to haul canoe and luggage across to Millinockett Stream. A mile of easy canoeing down this stream takes one into Shad Pond, the last "bulge" of any consequence on the river. Twelve miles of rapid water, accomplished in three hours, bring one to the mouth of the East Branch, whence it is twelve miles more to Mattawamkeag, where one takes the cars for Bangor.

By making the carry at Fowler's, one avoids twelve miles of very rapid water, and saves much time and labor. Grand Falls, on this part of the river, is about twelve or fifteen feet high, and can be visited most easily by paddling through Shad Pond and up the river for a mile and a half.

To the lover of scenery, this tour down the West Branch offers perhaps more attractions than any other in that part of Maine. There are, to be sure, many carries to make, but the wildness of the river, the picturesqueness of the lakes within easy access of it, and the grandeur of Mount Katahdin, which continually discovers some new feature, together form a combination of enjoyments seldom to be found.

RÉSUMÉ.

Chesuncook Lake to Dam . . . . 17m.
Dam to Ripogenus Carry . . . . 2¾m.
Ripogenus Carry . . . . 3m.
Ripogenus Carry to Ambajemackomus Carry . 2½m.
Ambajemackomus Carry to Sandy Stream . . 6½m.
Sandy Stream to Ambajejus Falls . . . . . 15m.

Ambajejus Falls to North Twin Dam . . . . 14m.
North Twin Dam to Shad Pond . . . . . 5m.
Shad Pond to Mattawamkeag . . . . . . 25m.

JO MARY LAKES.

There are three lakes in this chain, — West, South, and Big Jo Mary. The first, or West Jo Mary, lies southwest of the others, and is over half a mile from South Jo Mary. Canoes have to be carried across from one to the other. Between South and Big Jo Mary there is a thoroughfare of forty rods or more in length. At times the water in it is substantially "dead," — at others, quick.

From Big Jo Mary to Pamedomcook Lake is a mile and a half or more, by the stream, which is partly navigable by canoes. A good road runs from one lake to the other near the stream.

NAHMAKANTA LAKE

is most easily reached from Pamedomcook Lake. The stream which connects the two is about seven or eight miles long, and for two or three miles is navigable. Canoes and luggage will have to be carried about four miles over the old carry road, on the north side of the stream. The lake is a very attractive sheet of water some four miles long, and into its northern end flow two streams. The more easterly comes from

RAINBOW LAKE,

and is four miles long. Its water is "dead" for about a mile and a half from the mouth, up to a dam. Above

MILLINOKETT LAKE.

this point the stream is shallow, but the monotony is broken by several small ponds, which lessen one's labor considerably. A good road runs up the east side of the brook, and it may be advisable, if the water is low, to carry from the head of dead water to the lake. Rainbow Lake is considered one of the prettiest in the neighborhood, both from its own inherent charms, and from the fine views of surrounding mountains to be had from its shores, and from a ridge just north of it. If one follows up for two miles the other brook which empties into Nahmakanta Lake, one comes into Female Pond, whence it is easy to reach, by canoe, Pollywog and Muskrat Ponds, and to ascend for some distance the stream which comes from Penobscot and Wadleigh Ponds.

MILLINOKETT LAKE

is most easily reached from Ambajejus Lake, by a short carry which begins at the head of a grassy cove. The lake is very picturesque, and is studded with pretty islands, which, in combination with the glorious views of Katahdin and surrounding mountains, make it a very attractive spot for artists. No trout are in its waters, and the brook which is its outlet is about twelve miles long and unnavigable.

NORTHWEST CARRY.

Carry Brook, a small stream in which abound sunken logs, stumps, and snags, empties into the northwest arm of Moosehead Lake, in its upper left-hand corner, and to the left of Ferd. Lane's clearing. Paddling up this brook for nearly a mile, to the head of navigation, one comes to a landing on the left bank, from which one reaches, a few yards distant, the direct road from Lane's to Seeboomook Meadows. This road runs northwest, and for some distance covers the same ground as the Old Canada Road, which leads from Lane's to Canada Falls, and beyond to Canada.

From the landing to the meadows is a long mile and a half, the road being good, except after a rain, when the walking is soft. Ferd. Lane promptly appears at the landing with a horse and sled, if previously asked to do so, and hauls canoe and luggage across the carry, charging from a dollar and a half to two dollars per load.

Seeboomook Meadows consist of a small tract of ground lying near the West Branch, and the pond which covers a part of it, from a quarter to three eighths of a mile in diameter, is connected with the river by a shallow and narrow stream flowing northeasterly for a quarter of a mile from its east side.

WEST BRANCH OF THE PENOBSCOT.—SEEBOOMOOK FALLS.

This part of the river is pretty difficult of navigation, and parties find it easier and shorter to be hauled across the Northeast and Northwest Carries, and to paddle over the lake between them, than to attempt to accomplish the same distance on the river. A visit, however, to Seeboomook Falls is quite worth while, if one has the time.

Just below the foot of Seeboomook Island are the first

falls, past which, on the left, one must carry for a quarter of a mile. Two miles and a half of good canoeing follow, — good except in one place, the Dam Pitch, where one must lift one's craft over. Then come the long falls. At high water one must carry at least three quarters of a mile, in low water nearly double that distance, the path being on the right. Some three miles below the rapids is the mouth of Russell Stream, and from there to the Northeast Carry, or Morris farm, is two miles more. Seeboomook Falls is a wild and dangerous place, and the dread of log-drivers on the Upper Penobscot.

RUSSELL STREAM

is rather small, and for four miles, from its mouth up to the pond, rapid; but a canoe can be worked up its channel slowly. Above the pond the stream is dead, and crooked, for some miles. Russell Pond used to be good moose and caribou ground.

ELM STREAM.

A small island marks the mouth of Elm Stream, just above the lower Seeboomook Falls. For twelve miles, up to Elm Pond, the brook is substantially dead water, but, being choked in many places by logs and trees, is practically unnavigable.

WEST BRANCH OF THE PENOBSCOT, GOING UP FROM NORTHWEST CARRY.

Opposite the mouth of Seeboomook Stream, on Seeboomook Island, is a good camp-ground. The river here is black and deep, a character it maintains for some seven miles above, as far as Swan's farm, and is in places very picturesque.

A half-mile brings one to the head of the island, above which the river widens considerably, and after another mile and a half Nelhudus Stream is reached. This brook has two mouths, one natural and the other artificial, and is navigable for some distance. Good fishing is to be had, late in the summer, in pools here and there among its windings.

From the opposite or right bank of the river, just below Nelhudus, a good tote-road leads into the Old Canada Road, — it being about six miles from the river to Lane's.

From Nelhudus five miles of paddling, past picturesque Camp Pocahontas and around several sharp bends in the river, bring one to Swan's farm, on the left. On the high bank, along which at the west end of the clearing leads the path to Swan's "shanty," is a convenient camping-ground, without, however, a very bountiful supply of good fire-wood.

Above Swan's the river for half a mile is shallow and the current strong, rendering it necessary, in low water, to wade and to drag canoes. At the end of this half-mile is the first or lowest pitch of Gulliver Falls, between which and the next pitch — a few rods — Gulliver Stream empties into the river on the right. The second pitch is at the foot of a small island, going to the left of which one soon passes up over the third pitch, — the head of the rapids. In moderately high water two men can take a loaded canoe up over these rapids without much difficulty; but in low water resort must be had to the dragging process.

Two miles and a half of deep "dead" water intervene between the head of Gulliver Falls and the foot of Big Island, passing up the right side of which, five eighths of a mile, to the head, one comes to open land, and to more shallow and in some places " strong " water. The passage around the left of the island is narrower, and a quarter of a mile longer.

On the left, a few rods above the island, is the mouth of a "logon," pushing up which for forty rods a pool will be found encircled by lily-pads, where small trout are abundant.

From Big Island a mile of paddling brings one to King's High Landing, where from ledges on the left there is also good fishing. From this point it is less than a mile to Knights's farm and shanty, at the forks of the North and South Branches, where the canoe-man's hard work begins in earnest.

RÉSUMÉ.

Lane's to mouth of Seeboomook Brook . . . . . 3m.
Mouth of Seeboomook Brook to Nelhudus Stream . 2m.
Nelhudus Stream to Swan's Shanty . . . . . . 5m.
Swan's Shanty to head of Gulliver Falls . . . . . ¾m.
Gulliver Falls to head of Big Island . . . . . . 3¼m.
Big Island to Knights's, — the Forks . . . . . . 2m.

It takes from five to six hours to go from Lane's across the carry, and up the river as far as Swan's, and from four to five hours from Swan's to the forks. In low water it may take the better part of a day to accomplish the latter distance.

SOUTH BRANCH OF THE PENOBSCOT.

Leaving the forks, and ascending the South Branch (much narrower than the main river), a mile and a half of swift water over a bed of rocks, in places so thickly strewn as to render the passage of a canoe almost impossible, bring one to the foot of Canada Falls. More or less wading will be found unavoidable over this stretch, except in high water, the worst part being immediately below the falls. The river here makes a very marked bend, having flowed for two miles and a half in almost a semicircle northwards, and then sweeping off at a sharp angle towards the east. Canada Falls consists of a succession of deep, narrow gorges, down and through which the water froths and roars. This part of the river is well worth seeing; but to take through it a loaded canoe, by alternate dragging and carrying, will require the better part of a long day. It takes much less time to make the long carry — a mile and a half — over the Old Canada Road, which leaves the foot of the falls, runs up the steep bank, then southwest by south, and at the end of three eighths of a mile turns sharply to the right. A mile and a half over a good road, hard and dry except in one place, is a pleasant substitute for an all-day's journey along and through the river. Put in at a dam at the head of the falls, and after a long half-mile through a very rocky stream, and past one "pitch" where the "painter," or leading-rope, will be needed, another dam marks the place where smooth and deep water finally becomes a reality.

On the left bank just above the foot of the falls, and again just above the head of the falls, cold-water brooks will be found.

From the upper and larger dam it is half a mile to Bog Brook. Until well away from the dam, look out for large rocks just under water.

Passing by Bog Brook, which seems to be the sluggish outlet of a small bog about a quarter of a mile from the river, one paddles two miles, — the latter of which is around an ox-bow, — and bending sharply to the west, comes to the mouth of Alder Brook. Up the river, about a mile from here, is the mouth of Hale Brook, opposite which is a flat ledge projecting halfway across the stream, and below the ledge a deep pool, where trout of medium size abound. A good camp-ground lies just over this ledge. It affords plenty of hard wood and good water, and the hunting-grounds of Alder Brook are conveniently near it. A "logon," a few rods up the river on the same side, is a favorite feeding-ground for ducks. A logging-camp back of the "logon" will afford dingy shelter to parties not provided with a tent, and cool brook-water is near at hand. A good road runs back from this camp to the Old Canada Road, which it joins about a mile from the river.

A few rods above Hale Brook the character of the river banks changes, from a densely wooded to an open grassy elm-land, which character they maintain for a mile and a half. The sportsman's course is generally west; and two miles from Hale Brook, the water begins to be shallow in places, over which wading and dragging may be necessary. A mile and a quarter of this sort of navigation gives place to a mile of shallow, rock-strewn, dead water separated into two stretches by a short interval of quick water, and then for two miles more follow a succession of pools alternating with gravel and sand bars, when the mouth of Penobscot Brook is reached. This small stream, about five feet wide, flows out of Penobscot Lake, several miles through swampy ground, is choked up with fallen trees, and is entirely unnavigable. Its volume of water is about one fourth that of Bald Brook, which properly is the Penobscot, and should so be called.

Above this point canoeing is out of the question, excepting, perhaps, immediately after a very heavy rain, when, by dint of energetic poling, a canoe might ascend this boulder-strewn stream to a piece of "dead" water and alder ground, a mile or more above the junction of the two brooks. A tote-road, however, follows the stream, on its right bank, beginning three miles or more below Penobscot Brook, and becomes quite good a short distance above it. It crosses several ridges, and passes three decayed logging-camps, until, bearing off to the south, to the west of Bald Mountain, it finally joins the Canada Road in Sandy Bay township.

Penobscot Lake is best reached by taking to the Old Canada Road, and carrying canoe and load over it, from some point on the river near the road. The road, be it said, above the old camp near Hale Brook, has not been much used of late years, and is therefore "grown up" in places.

RÉSUMÉ.

Forks of North and South Branches to Canada Falls . 1½m.
Foot of Canada Falls to Upper Dam . . . . . . 2m.
Upper Dam to Penobscot Brook . . . . 10m.

It takes about five hours to go from the Forks to the upper dam, and from six to seven hours more to the mouth of Penobscot Brook.

ALDER BROOK,

twenty years ago a favorite feeding-ground for moose, runs through a stretch of country for the most part open and flat, and affording the best opportunity in the neighborhood for "still-hunting." Long grass covers its banks, with plenty of alder-bushes and some scrubby willows interspersed. For about two miles a canoe can run up the stream with ease, the general direction being south, and, beyond that point, west. The writer, on his only visit to this brook, in 1878, found a new beaver-dam about two miles from its mouth, which so raised the water as to render the passage very good for nearly a mile and a half further. The water above the dam was so deep, however, that he does not hesitate to express an opinion that very little difficulty in ascending the stream would be met by the canoe-man, even in the absence of such a dam. Good camping-ground will be found on the right, just below a short piece of shallow water, over which the canoe must be carried. Above these "rips" the stream is deep again for a mile, followed by a mile of shallow and deep places alternating. An old "landing" is at the foot of the quick water, which now appears in earnest, and here the canoe must stop, unless the brook should be high. The bed of the stream above this point is very rocky, and continues so for a mile and a half to an old dam. On the right a road leads up the stream, at the landing blindly to be sure, but above the dam it opens out and affords good walking up to, and beyond, a ridge which runs north to the pond. The brook above the dam appears to be dead for about two miles and a half, its course being nearly east. It comes from the pond southerly, three quarters of a mile, to the point where the road crosses it; the latter goes a quarter of a mile further before it reaches the ridge spoken of above. Along the top of this ridge is a good path. The water of the pond is not cold, and the locality seems to promise little, either for fish or for game. Bald Mountain lies four or five miles southwest.

This excursion, from the mouth of the brook to the pond and back, can be made comfortably in one day.

NORTH BRANCH OF THE PENOBSCOT.

The ascent of this stream is difficult and slow, at and from its very junction with the South Branch. Wide and shallow, it flows over bars of gravel and sand, which lie a few rods apart and separate stretches of deceptively smooth water. Large rocks strewn thickly over the bottom make it difficult to find a channel for even a lightly laden canoe.

From the forks to Big Lane Brook, on the left, is about a mile and a half; thence three quarters of a mile to Leadbetter Brook on the same side; thence three quarters of a mile to an old camp (Spencer's) on the right, and from there to Leadbetter Falls, about three quarters of a mile further, — or nearly four miles in all.

Leadbetter Falls consists of several short pitches, over which a canoe can be pulled up or let down by the "painter" without much trouble, except, perhaps, in high water, when they can be run, coming down, on the paddle. The carry is only a few rods long, and lies on the right, going up. The tote-road follows the river here, and as far up as High Landing, two miles above, where one branch leaves it and runs north and northeast, until it again nears it within three miles of the foot of Abacotnetic Bog. The other branch follows the stream up to the mouth of Dole Brook.

The river immediately above the falls is somewhat deeper, and navigation a trifle easier. Three and a half miles from the falls one comes opposite West Green Mountain, pleasing glimpses of which are had from time to time, from below. There are now more stretches of dead water, and the stream grows perceptibly narrower. Up to this point it has seemed shut in, as it were, and its banks have been lined for the most part with soft-wood ridges. Now, however, the country grows more open, and hard wood predominates, while the rocky character of the river-bed changes for several miles to that of sand and gravel.

A few minutes' walk brings one in sight of East Green Mountain, a half-mile higher up the stream, which at its base winds abruptly from the west, and the canoeman's course tends more northwesterly. Following, for a mile, a ridge which descends from the western mountain northerly, one comes to an island half a mile long, on the left side of which, going up, will be found the better channel. From the head of the island it is about a mile to the mouth of Dole Brook, fifty rods below which, in a deep pool, good fishing will be found.

Three miles more bring one to the mouth of Norris Brook, from which to the foot of the Alder Ground is about nine miles. Abacotnetic "Lake" is a narrow sheet of water with boggy shores, and is about a mile long. Of its sluggish character and appearance the stream partakes for four or five miles below the outlet. From the end of the dead-water, however, to the mouth of Dole Brook, there is hardly any water at all, and, difficult of passage as are the ten miles below Dole Brook, the navigation immediately above it is still more difficult and almost impossible. Indeed, it is only after a hard and continuous rain of a day or two, or during a wet season, that the ascent of the North Branch is accomplished at all, and that too by hard pushing.

In the absence of high water, wading, and dragging of canoes will be the order of the day, with scarcely any intermission, — a process tiresome to the voyager, and ruinous to the canoe.

Except in the pool already mentioned, and possibly in some others nearer Green Mountains, and in one a mile below them, there is little fishing in this stream. Caribou and deer abound just below Dole Brook, and caribou are plenty around Abacotnetic Bog.

The road from the Forks to the bog, after leaving High Landing, runs a mile and a quarter to Spencer's camp of 1878-9; thence five and a half miles to Truesdell and Hildreth's camp (1878-9), which is at the east end of a shallow pond, about a mile and a half from the mouth of Norris Brook. It soon descends a steep hill, crosses a cedar swamp, and runs over another long hill, a mile from the foot of which is Spencer's camp of 1877-8, partly burnt. The road goes to the left of the camp, northwest, towards the stream, which is about a quarter of a mile away. From this camp it is two miles to the end of the carry to St. John Pond, and two miles more to the head of the bog, the road skirting around it at some distance from the water, to avoid soft ground.

RÉSUMÉ.

Forks to Leadbetter Falls . . . . 4m.
Falls to Dole Brook . . . . 6m.
Dole Brook to Norris Brook . . . . 3m.
Norris Brook to Alder Ground . . . . . . 9m.
Alder Ground to Head of Bog . . . . . . 5m.

Ordinarily it will take two days to go from the Forks to Dole Brook. Beyond that point it is impossible to give an estimate of time. It might take a day to reach the bog, or it might take a week.

DOLE BROOK,

or Middle Branch, will be found generally impracticable of navigation, and, aside from the falls, of little interest, either by way of scenery or promise of game. The main fall is about a mile and a half from the mouth of the brook. The water here trickles down the rock about ten or twelve feet. An eighth of a mile above, there is quite a long ledge, which slopes from the left bank to the centre of the stream, and forms its bed in times of freshets. It is worn into all sorts of basins and fissures and odd shapes, by the action of the water.

At high water, that part of the stream above the falls will not present many obstacles to the canoe-man, and is chiefly used, at such seasons, either by lumbermen or smugglers. A tote-road runs from the mouth of the brook, on the north side, to Canada. It is as a whole quite good, lying through groves of soft wood, "burnt-slash," and over hard-wood ridges. It runs pretty near the brook as far as the falls, then half-way over the "slash" nears it again, soon leaves it a second time, however, and, veering to the north, meets an old road (Lee's) from Dole Pond to the upper North Branch. Here it turns at a sharp angle, leads southwest and west, and again comes out to the stream just below Dole Pond. Plunging again into the woods, and crossing Robert Brook, one soon comes out at an old clearing. The old storehouse, the skeleton of which still remains standing on the bank of the pond, was built years ago, when lumbering was good in this region. Supplies were brought here from Canada, and grain and hay raised on the clearing during the summer, and distributed in winter to the neighboring lumbermen.

DOLE POND,

about a mile and a half long, and one mile broad in its widest part, is shallow and uninteresting, as is also Frost Pond, its counterpart, two and a half miles beyond. Between the two is an extensive "logon" frequented by caribou. No thoroughfare connects this "logon" with Dole Pond, the stream in summer disappearing almost wholly in one place, in or beneath a bog.

RÉSUMÉ.

Mouth of Dole Brook to Falls	1½m.
Falls to Burnt Land	¾m.
Burnt Land	2m.
Burnt Land to Dam	4¼m.
Dam to Storehouse	¾m.
Storehouse to Frost Pond	3¼m.

There seem to be no fish in these ponds and streams.

LONG POND.

To the south of and emptying into Dole Pond by a small stream navigable in high water, and about two miles in length, lies Long Pond, a charming little sheet of water between two and three miles long, and varying in breadth from a half-mile to a mile. It is shut in by high wooded hills on every side, and seems to be quite deep. There is said to be good fishing in its waters.

ST. JOHN POND

is an attractive sheet of water about three miles long, and a mile or more broad. It is reached from the North Branch of the Penobscot, by a good carry two miles and forty-four rods long, which leaves that stream at an old "landing" on a rather low but steep bank. The end of the carry is about ten minutes' walk below the mouth of a small brook on the same side, and seems to follow up the course of the brook until within a short distance of St. John Pond. Two brooks at the upper end of the pond afford good fishing. One of them is the outlet of seven small ponds, picturesquely ensconced among surrounding mountains. A canoe can penetrate almost to the first of these ponds, but the others are rather hard of access.

BAKER LAKE.

From Abacotnetic Bog, Baker Lake may be reached by two routes. The shorter route leads from a point a few rods up the brook which flows into the bog at its upper end. An old stump, some eight feet high, marks the place where the carry begins. Two miles of rather soft walking bring one to Baker *Brook*, down which a canoe can be propelled without much difficulty to Baker Bog, two miles and a half of the way being "dead" water. Between this bog-pond and Baker Lake, however, navigation is more difficult, and the water in the brook for nearly three miles "tumbles down hill," as the guides say, in a way that is discouraging.

The other route is by way of St. John Pond, whose outlet, the Woboostook or Baker *Stream*, flows eighteen miles, in an almost semicircular course, to Baker Lake. For six miles canoeing is said to be pretty good, then come about eight miles of carrying and dragging, between which and the lake are four miles of "dead" water.

The first of these routes is always preferable, because even in low water there is about one third as much carrying and dragging to be done over it as there is in the second, while in the latter some parts of the stream are choked by logs and driftwood; and when there is an abundance of water and good canoeing in one stream, there is also enough for as good canoeing in the other.

From Baker Lake there is "strong" water, but plenty of it, to Seven Islands, some sixty or seventy miles distant, from which place parties can be hauled across to Long Lake, on the Allagash, and come back to Moosehead by way of Chamberlain Lake and Mud Pond, or else descend the Allagash into the St. John again, thus avoiding the dangers of Black River Rapids.

Baker Lake has a good reputation for fish and game, which certainly ought to be abundant there, owing to the difficulty of reaching the place.

One day is enough in which to go from Abacotnetic Bog to Baker Lake, or two days from St. John Pond to the lake, and from that point Seven Islands may be reached in less than two days.

CAUCOMGOMOC LAKE

empties its waters through a stream of the same name, about twelve miles long, into Chesuncook Lake. With the exception of the upper three miles of the stream and two short falls, the water is smooth and navigation unrestricted. Until within a few years this region has been little visited, but from its accessibility and picturesqueness it is fast becoming a popular resort.

Leaving Chesuncook Lake, paddling about a mile, past the mouth of the Umbazooksus and over a small "rip," brings one to a miniature pond, at the northeast corner of which, to the left of the falls, is the end of a thirty-rod carry. There are two main pitches to these falls, some three and four feet high respectively. Putting in either at the head of the upper pitch, or further up the stream, around a bend at the foot of a very steep bank, a mile and a quarter intervene before the second fall is reached, — a single pitch of seven feet. Brandy Brook, between these two falls, furnishes good fishing after the first of September.

From the upper falls to Black Pond is a mile and a half, and across the pond a mile and a quarter more. Thus far the water is deep and black, and the river banks pretty wide apart. Beyond Black Pond the banks converge, the water is clearer, and a current is appreciable. For three and a half miles, past Little Scott Brook, no obstructions exist. At its mouth, and in the river above, trout may be taken in a number of places. Half a mile above this brook "rips" appear, two or three rods long, and here passengers will have to walk, and, in low water, carry canoes and baggage. At the foot of the bank, around the bend, is another good trout-hole.

Half a mile more brings one to the foot of the "horse-race," two and a half miles long, up which a canoe with a light load may be poled or dragged, without great difficulty, unless the water is very high or very low. There is only one place to be lifted over.

A good road runs from opposite Murphy's on Chesuncook Lake, up the Caucomgomoc River, touching it at the second falls, and again about three miles from Caucomgomoc Lake. The last two and a half miles of this road are excellent, being on high ground, and dry. Fishing may be had in a pool just below the outlet of the lake.

The lake is one of the prettiest spots in Maine. It is about seven miles long, and three miles broad at its widest part, is of irregular shape, and has several small islands at its upper end. A charming camping-ground will be found on either side of a small point of land, which juts out from the west shore, some five miles from the outlet. On the north and south sides of the point are long stretches of sand-beach, back of which is good level camping-ground and plenty of wood, and on the north an icy cold brook. From the south side the view is fine, taking in a wide expanse of blue water. On the north, the lake narrows considerably and the view is much more limited, being broken by pretty islands, and overshadowed, as it were, by forest-clad mountains on the west, — a decided contrast with the other view.

The shores of the lake are in many places rocky and covered with cedars, and, excepting at the upper end, offer few good camping-places.

AVERY BROOK

empties into the head of Caucomgomoc Lake, to the west of a broad piece of meadow-land and "logon." It comes from a small pond of the same name about a mile and a quarter distant, and varies in width from ten to thirty feet. For half a mile it is deep enough for a canoe, but for the rest of the way quite shallow, and will give abundant opportunity to wade, and perhaps to make two or three short carries over its bed. The pond is quite small and almost completely overgrown with sedge-grass and lilies, but contains an inexhaustible supply of small trout, which rise freely in the morning and evening. Good fishing may also be had at the mouth of Avery Brook.

LOON LAKE

is even prettier than its neighbor, but much more difficult of access. It is quite deep, and some three miles long by from one to two miles broad. Its outlet into Caucomgomoc Lake is a shallow and rocky stream about four miles long, hard to navigate even at high water. A good road runs along the south bank, beginning at the head of the dead-water (a half-mile from the mouth of the stream). It soon passes an old logging camp, crosses the brook three quarters of a mile above it, and runs direct to the lower end of the lake, some two miles further.

HURD PONDS

are connected with Loon Lake by narrow and unnavigable brooks a few rods long. The lower pond is quite pretty, but the second one is shallow, and its shores dreary and uninviting.

ROUND POND.

On the other side of Caucomgomoc Lake, and connected with it by a deep stream (called the "Sis," abbreviated from Caucomgomocsis or Little Caucomgomoc) three miles long, and rocky only at its mouth, is Round Pond, a body of water a mile and a half

long by one mile wide Good camping-ground will be found on the northwest side of the pond at the foot of a hard-wood ridge, or on the northeast side. Good fishing may be had in a spring hole near the mouth of a small brook on this latter side, or at the mouth of, and in, Poland Brook.

DAGGETT POND

is connected with Round Pond by a small stream a mile and a half long, through which at high water a canoe can easily be paddled. A beaver dam at the mouth of this stream for several years kept back enough water to answer all the purposes of the canoe-man going to Daggett Pond. This sheet of water, about a mile and a half in diameter, offers no special attractions except, perhaps, in the way of cranberries, which grow in profusion on its northwest and southwest sides.

A mile and a half intervene between Daggett Pond and Shallow Lake, the connecting stream being too small for a canoe, but furnishing good walking in its bed for three quarters of a mile, past a miniature fall, to an old dam. Above this dam a canoe can be led and carried to a second dam, and from there paddled among sharp rocks to

SHALLOW LAKE,

whose shores on nearly all its sides are swampy and covered with grass and hackmatack growth.

The lake is about two miles long and a mile and a quarter broad, and with the exception of a part, about a mile in diameter, towards its eastern end, is only from six inches to a foot deep, and covered with lily-pads and sedge-grass. The bottom is mud unadulterated, and the waves and ripples made by the progress of a canoe will bring bubbles of gas in great quantities to the surface of the water, on all sides, even *ahead* of the canoe.

The lake lies diagonally north and south, and has two small islands at its west central end. A good road leads from its eastern extremity to Chamberlain Lake.

Black ducks are found here in great quantities, and cranberries are plenty. At the northwest end of the lake, near the outlet, there runs along the shore a natural ridge about four feet high, a sort of embankment, behind which the land falls two or three feet again. There are no trout in Shallow Lake, but some have been taken at the mouth of Shallow Lake brook in Daggett Pond. The boggy shores of both ponds are cut up with caribou tracks.

POLAND BROOK

for a quarter of a mile from its mouth is deep, this character then giving place for another quarter-mile to a succession of "rips" and shallow places, through which some wading must be done. A miniature fall of three feet marks the reappearance of smooth water, which extends up to Poland Pond. Above the falls the stream widens considerably, and on either side are hackmatack bogs covered with grass and low bushes. Lily-pads cover the water except in the middle of the stream. These features predominate for two miles.

The stream then resumes its old appearance, narrows a good deal, and exchanges a muddy for a sandy and rocky bottom. One mile more brings one to

POLAND POND,

a pleasing little sheet of water about three quarters of a mile long and half a mile broad. There is some swampy ground at its western end, which makes islands of two pieces of high land jutting out into the pond. A narrow channel which runs through this swamp leads over a succession of beaver dams, to quite an extensive beaver pond.

Wadleigh Brook, which empties into the northern end of the pond, is clear and cold, and at times affords good fishing.

Parties who wish to visit and explore this region can best do so by camping on Round Pond, and taking one day for Poland Pond, and one for Shallow Lake and Daggett Pond. A light load, consisting of provisions for two days, an axe, kettle, frying-pan, and blankets, can be taken from there with canoe to Allagash Lake, and a very pleasant and easy excursion made.

RÉSUMÉ.

Chesuncook Lake to Caucomgomoc Lake	12m.
Caucomgomoc Lake, length	7m.
Caucomgomoc Lake to Loon Lake	4m.
Caucomgomoc Lake to Round Pond	3m.
Caucomgomoc Lake to Avery Pond	1¼m.
Round Pond to Poland Pond	3½m.
Round Pond to Shallow Lake	4½m.

It takes about a day to go from Chesuncook Lake to Caucomgomoc Lake. The carry around the "horse-race" can easily be made, canoe and baggage, in three hours.

ALLAGASH LAKE.

At the head of the dead-water near the mouth of Poland Brook begins the carry which leads to Allagash Lake. The path runs along a ridge of low mountains, perhaps half or one third of the way up their sides, and is three miles long and quite dry and open. From the end of the carry it is about three miles around to the mouth of Allagash Stream, a quiet, cold, narrow, and deep brook, with a sandy and rocky bottom, and navigable for several miles with comparative ease. There are no rapids, and but few "rips," for some distance from its mouth, but the current is quite strong. The stream, not having been "driven" of late years, is, higher up, somewhat choked with logs and drift wood. At and near its mouth there is good fishing.

The northeast shore of the lake is low and sandy, that on the west is rocky, and often precipitous to a height of fifty or seventy-five feet. West of the lake several mountains, the Toulbah range, appear quite strikingly; the country on the other sides, however, is flat and uninteresting.

Several small brooks empty into Allagash Lake, none of which are navigable. Good camping-ground may be found on the west side of the lake about a mile from the inflowing Allagash, beneath a precipitous wall of rock.

Parties sometimes ascend Allagash Stream to Mud Pond, and carrying across, over an old road, to Chemquasabamticook (pronounced Jim-se-bem-se-cook) Lake, go down the stream of that name into Long Lake.

Chamberlain Lake may be reached by going down the Allagash. The stream is rapid for about two miles and a half, to Allagash Pond. Below the pond, half a mile or more, there is a fall. Then, for a mile, rapid and "dead" water alternate, as far as another fall, between which and the lake there is half a mile of smooth water. In places the water is quite rough, and, where carrying is necessary, the paths, having of late years been little used, are obstructed by a thick undergrowth of bushes. However, when the water is moderately high, no very great difficulty will be encountered in going either down or up the stream.

DOWN THE ST. JOHN RIVER.

The first part of this route has already been described on pages 62 and 63.

From the head of Chesuncook Lake, and mouth of Caucomgomoc Stream, it is but a fraction of a mile to the mouth of the Umbazooksus, — a stream which for three or four miles winds sluggishly, but with provoking pertinacity, through low meadow-lands which yield a yearly abundance of hay to the Chesuncook farmers. There is a cold spring on the right about a mile from the mouth of the stream. Above this stretch of "dead" water there is quick and shallow water for a mile and a half, or more, through which a canoe may be poled, or led, without much difficulty, except for perhaps a quarter of a mile, where carrying may become necessary. A good road runs on the right up to Umbazooksus Lake.

Paddling a mile across the southeast corner of the lake, one comes to the beginning of the famous Mud Pond Carry, the dread of guides, and abomination of sportsmen. This carry is two miles long, and in many places has the appearance of the bed of a brook, with water and mud enough almost to float a canoe. Except in very dry seasons the traveller here sinks in mire up to his ankles, and without a pair of rubber boots is indeed "at sea." This hardship once over, the rest of the St. John trip is so comparatively easy and pleasant, that the remembrance of one's toil is soon lost, for the time, in keen enjoyment.

MUD POND,

whose name carries with it its chief characteristic, is nearly round, and about a mile wide. Lifting over a dam at its outlet, wading again becomes necessary for about a mile down the brook, which for a mile or more near its mouth broadens into a sort of "logon," where ducks congregate. A run of two miles and a half across

CHAMBERLAIN LAKE

brings one to Chamberlain farm, where the most necessary articles of camp fare are usually to be had.

The shores of this lake are very unattractive. Some years ago a large dam was built at its natural outlet, and the water forced back and through an artificial "cut" or canal between Telos and Webster Lakes. This enables the lumberman to take his logs down the East Branch of the Penobscot River to a home market, instead of having to go into New Brunswick. The consequent rise of water in the lake flooded its shores and killed the trees on them for several yards back. Some of the withered trunks still stand with bare arms, in marked contrast to their living neighbors, while others have fallen, and help to make impenetrable any camping-ground which may be within. The tourist gladly passes on to the dam and lock, some three miles and a half from the farm. Two short carries must be made past these obstacles, — on the right, — and after running through some quick water and a pleasing little lakelet, one emerges into

EAGLE LAKE.

This is a pretty and irregular sheet of water, with attractive shores, and contains two or three good-sized islands. Several brooks empty into it, which are partially navigable, and through some of which access may be had to ponds beyond.

SMITH BROOK,

the outlet of Haymock Lake, is smooth water for three miles or more from its mouth, to the head of an island, and pretty broad in places. About four miles up, there are some falls and shoal water, past which, on the left, canoes must be carried, and above which "dead" water again appears.

Russell, Soper, Snare, and Thoroughfare Brooks are navigable for some distance, and afford good fishing in places, one of which is off a sandy point at the head of a small pond or "bulge" in Snare Brook.

From the locks to Eagle Lake Narrows is about ten miles, and to Thoroughfare Brook six miles more.

CHURCHILL LAKE

is about six miles long and three or four broad in its widest part. Into it empty the Twin Brooks. An old and difficult carry of about two miles and a half leads to Spider Lake on the right of the brook, beginning in a piece of burnt land, or second growth. A canoe can be put into the brook just below

SPIDER LAKE.

This is quite a pretty sheet of water, deep and surrounded mostly by high ground. A short carry leads to a pond just south of it. A succession of carries and ponds begin at its northeastern corner, and lead eventually into Munsungan Lake, and thence down into the Aroostook River.

At the foot of Churchill Lake are the remains of

CHASE'S DAM,

burnt, it is said, by parties from New Brunswick, who were angry at the prospect of losing all advantages which might accrue to them from logs which would otherwise naturally be sent down the river from Eagle and Churchill Lake waters. It is hardly necessary to say, that it was intended by means of this dam to raise the water, so that it would be level with that of Chamberlain Lake, when logs could pass south, instead of having to go down the Allagash.

At the dam begins, on the left, Chase's Carry, where it is expedient for such persons, at least, as are novices in the management of a canoe, to carry both their canoe and luggage. They thus avoid the Devil's Elbow, one of the worst places in the river, where in the midst of rocks and foaming water a canoe must shoot across from one side of the stream to the other, or swamp. The carry is about three quarters of a mile long. Immediately below it the water is quite rough for some little distance, and one must be continually on the alert to avoid shipwreck. This over, however, a canoe glides smoothly down the river past meadowland and grassy islands into Umsaskis Lake, — some eight or nine miles, in all.

From here, continuing through Long Lake, sixteen miles, to the Depot Farm, through which passes the road from Seven Islands, one paddles ten miles more into Square Lake. No obstacles to rapid progress intervene between Square Lake and Allagash Falls, — twenty miles, — nor between the latter and Grand Falls, on the St. John, about one hundred miles apart.

Allagash Falls are a mile or more below a point where the river widens, and where there are a number of islands. A farm-house (formerly M'Clellan's) stands on the right bank, opposite the head of this "bulge."

At the falls there are two carries, on the right, or rather one carry, part of which in high water need not be used. The river here, however, is full of sharp-pointed rocks, and great care must be taken to avoid them.

The falls are quite pretty, and consist of one broken, ragged, narrow pitch, some thirty feet or more high. The water, as it passes over it, is almost as white as milk. The carry is short. It is about twelve miles from the falls to the mouth of the Allagash, thirty-two more to Fort Kent, twenty more to the mouth of the Madawaska River, and thirty-seven more to Grand Falls.

Two or three days will take one to Grand Falls, where canoe and luggage will be hauled past the rapids, for a dollar or two.

The falls are some sixty feet high, one unbroken pitch, followed for a short distance by lesser falls and swirling hissing rapids. A pretty suspension bridge spans the chasm below the falls, and from it one obtains a charming view of the latter.

From Grand Falls it is about twenty-seven miles to Tobique, twenty more to Florenceville, and twenty more to Woodstock.

Two days are all that is required to paddle from Grand Falls to Woodstock, where one can continue by canoe, or, in high water, by steamer, seventy miles to Fredericton, thence a hundred miles to St. John, and thence by steamer to Portland or Boston. By rail one can reach St. John, a hundred and fifty miles, or, in the other direction, Bangor, in one day.

The last week spent on this trip is apt to be monotonous. The river banks present the same scenes, day after day, and at the mouth of the Allagash one feels that he has left the *woods* behind him, and is rapidly nearing home.

Fishing will be found in the Allagash in different places between Chase's dam and the junction with the St. John.

RÉSUMÉ.

Greenville or Kineo to Moosehorn	28–48m.
Umbazooksus Lake	20m.
Chamberlain Lock	1cm.
Thoroughfare Brook, or Chase's Carry	16–22m.
Umsaskis Lake, or Long Lake	9–25m.
Allagash Falls	30m.
Madawaska	64m.
Grand Falls	37m.
Woodstock	67m.
	323m.

The above table makes no allowance for delay caused by rain, low water, or for stops made for recreation.

EAST BRANCH OF THE PENOBSCOT.

The route from Moosehead to Chamberlain Lake has been previously described, on pages 101 and 102.

Near the upper end of Chamberlain Lake, at the "heel of the boot," is the natural *mouth* of a stream which now flows back into Telosmis (Little Telos Lake). The water in this stream is "dead," and a canoe passes easily into and across Telosmis and Telos Lake, some five miles, to the "cut" which was made some years ago to connect the latter body of water with Webster Lake. A canoe can run through this canal, which is over a mile long, at almost any time in summer, and without great difficulty. The water is quite rapid, but sufficiently deep for purposes of navigation.

WEBSTER LAKE

is about two miles long and perhaps half as wide. It furnishes good camping-ground and capital fishing. The brook, which is its outlet, is a very turbulent stream, and on its course of ten miles there are a great many "pitches" and falls, around which canoes must be carried. They are mostly short stretches, with no regular carry-paths, and in many cases all that is necessary is to lift over a ledge. The principal carry, and the last one on the brook, is about three quarters of a mile long, and lies on the left bank.

A short run below it takes one into

SECOND LAKE,

where Webster Brook joins the main East Branch. Three miles across this lake, and about as far again through the river, which is nearly all "dead" water, bring one into

GRAND LAKE.

There is a farm near the mouth of Trout Brook. Five miles across the lake bring one to the dam at its foot. At this point appear a range of mountains on the southwest, which give one the impression of following the tourist, as it were, in his course down the river for six or eight miles, from which circumstance they take their name, — the Traveller Mountains.

Below Grand Lake navigation is very much like that of Webster Brook, except that it is less difficult. The stretches of "dead" water are longer, and the rapids are deeper and less dangerous. Besides several smaller ones, there are two principal falls, between the lake and the junction of the river with the West Branch. The first is about fifteen miles below Grand Lake, and is known as Grand Falls. It extends over considerable ground, and in its course there are four "pitches," around which canoes must be carried. The other carry is about a mile long and on the right bank, about twelve miles from the mouth of the stream. It runs around the Grindstone Falls. From the junction of the East and West Branches in Medway it is twelve miles to Mattawamkeag.

For wildness of scenery this route surpasses even that down the West Branch, and is perhaps more difficult. It has the charm, moreover, of being seldom visited by tourists, and offers many a good trout pool, and not infrequently an opportunity to secure large game.

EBEEME PONDS AND PLEASANT RIVER.

Leaving the cars of the Bangor and Piscataquis Railroad at Milo, one takes stage five miles north to Brownville, whence leads a good stage-road, fourteen miles, through some interesting slate quarries, to Katahdin Iron-Works. A mile beyond Brownville, a branch road leads to Schoodic Lake, and also into a good logging road, which in turn runs past Lower Ebeeme (pronounced Eb-ee-my) Ponds, to Jo Mary Lakes. A pair of horses can haul canoes and luggage through from Brownville to West Jo Mary Lake in one day.

The upper and lower Ebeeme ponds lie about four miles apart, measured on the east branch of Pleasant River, which flows through them before its junction with the other branches. A canoe can be paddled and poled up the connecting stream for two miles without much difficulty, but above that point will have to be carried half a mile, and poled the rest of the way to the upper pond. The ponds and surrounding country are quite picturesque, several wooded mountain peaks being near at hand on either side.

The lower group of ponds consists of West Ebeeme, connected by a narrow thoroughfare with Horseshoe Pond, into which empties, by a small brook on the north, Pearl Pond, and on the east, East Ebeeme Pond, the latter being three quarters of a mile from Schoodic Lake, and connected with it by a good path. There are numerous coves and inlets around the shores of these ponds, which, besides being pretty, make good shooting-ground. A good farm, cultivated by Elisha Norton, lies on the Jo Mary road near Schoodic Lake.

Into the Upper Ebeeme empties, on the north, Wangen Brook, which for two miles from its mouth is navigable by canoes. From the head of the dead water a good road leads into the Jo Mary road, and it is only four miles to Jo Mary Lake.

Horace Falls, two miles above Upper Ebeeme, is a pretty little cascade fifteen feet or more high, with a small island perched in the middle of it.

Persons who visit Ebeeme Ponds leave the stage at the house of William Tufts, seven miles from Brownville.

KATAHDIN IRON-WORKS.

This township is northwest of Brownville, and the focus of the mining operations carried on in it is at a small pond east of Ore Mountain. Fifty men are employed at the furnace, whose annual capacity is about thirty-five hundred tons.

A small hotel, which is soon to be enlarged so as to accommodate seventy-five people, stands in the neighborhood of the furnace, and from it good fishing-grounds and picturesque resorts are of easy access. It is four miles to the top of Horseback Mountain, and the same distance to the top of Chairback, from each of which fine views may be had. The principal fishing-grounds are Little Houston Pond, two miles; Big Houston, three and a quarter miles; Houston Dead Water, two miles; East and West Chairback Ponds, six and seven miles respectively; Long Pond and Spruce Mountain Pond, each eight miles. Mummer-Nummer-Laugen Pond is in sight of the house, and the Mineral Springs are a mile from it.

From Katahdin Iron-Works the road leads north, past B Pond, which is ten miles away. There is said to be good trout-fishing here, and at one time caribou frequented the shores of the pond in large droves.

A branch road leads west from the Iron-Works for six miles, along the west branch of Pleasant River, nearly to the foot of the "Gulf," where for three miles or more the river passes through a wild and narrow gorge, highly picturesque, and of wonderful formation. In low water, one can follow up the stream, to a certain extent, along the water's edge, and get a good idea of this natural phenomenon. A good road also leads to Houston Ponds.

On the east branch of Pleasant River, above Upper Ebeeme Pond, is a similar gorge called the "Gauntlet," very wild, but not quite equal to the "Gulf." A tote-road runs from Lower Ebeeme Pond, from the mouth of Babel Brook to the Gauntlet, which is also four miles from Horace Falls.

Crawford and Cedar Ponds lie near an old obscure path called "Caribou Road," which branches off from the Jo Mary Road, a few miles south of Jo Mary Lake. Both ponds are hard of access, but the former furnishes good trout-fishing. A fine view of the surrounding mountains and lakes can be had from Cedar Mountain.*

SEBEC LAKE,

an oddly shaped body of water, and a very pretty one, lies near the line of the Bangor and Piscataquis Railroad, and can be reached conveniently by either of three routes. The first is by way of South Sebec, the second lies through Foxcroft, and the third begins at Abbot, — all stations on the Bangor and Piscataquis Railroad.

From South Sebec to Sebec Corner is a mile, and thence it is four miles to Sebec Village, at the extreme east end of the lower lake, or pond. Stages connect with the regular trains, and the fare to the village is twenty-five cents.

* For guides, and information about this region, address Luther M. Gerrish, Brownville, Me.

At Foxcroft one can go by stage, or private conveyance, at 7 A. M., due north four miles and a half to Blethen Landing, at the west end of the lower pond. There is a small mill here, as well as several farm-houses where one can get a meal if needed, and await the arrival of the steamer, which is due at 8 : 15 A. M. The fare from Foxcroft to the head of the lake is fifty cents, or about a dollar if by private conveyance. The road from Abbot runs nine miles to the Lake House, at the mouth of Wilson Stream.

Blueberries grow in profusion near the lake, and during the time when they are ripe a small steamer makes the round trip up and down the lake every day, and runs pretty regularly during the rest of the summer season, — say from July 25th to September 1st, — leaving Sebec Village in the morning, and returning from Wilson Stream in the afternoon. Campers-out will find guides, canoes, and the ordinary articles of an outfit at Sebec Village, and all at reasonable prices. Good guides charge about a dollar and a half a day for their services, including canoe. Sail-boats, canoes, and tents are to let at the village, where Mr. Frank M. Ford will attend to the wants of sportsmen.

In the spring, when the ice first breaks up, the fishing at Sebec Lake is very good. Land-locked salmon abound in its waters, and furnish capital sport to the angler. They average about two and a half pounds in weight, and are very "gamy," sometimes leaping out of water two feet or more. People may be disappointed who visit the lake in summer or autumn, expecting to catch them right and left ; but after having learned their habits, one can reasonably expect to be well repaid for a visit of a fortnight. In July and August pickerel and white-perch are the fish caught most abundantly in the lake.

The lake is twelve miles long altogether, its lower arm six miles long and averaging a hundred and fifty rods wide, and its upper or larger part about four miles from east to west. It is surrounded by high ridges, among which Pine, Birch, Slate, and Granite Mountains rise here and there into prominence, and give an air of wildness to its lovely bays and dark blue waters.

Besides the lake proper there are a number of ponds and streams near by, which contain trout in abundance. A. G. Crockett's hotel, the Lake House, is situated near the mouth of Wilson Stream, and from it a good wagon-road leads three miles through a small settlement, to within three quarters of a mile of Grindstone Pond, one of the favorite fishing-grounds. Wilson Stream is navigable for about a mile from its mouth. Parties who wish to go over into Buck's Cove can save paddling some three miles by carrying a few rods over Uncle Jim's Carry, just east of Wilson Stream. Some persons think of building a house for sportsmen, this season, near the mouth of Ship Pond Stream. If the plan is carried out, it will doubtless result successfully, as Buck's Cove is one of the best localities on the lake for land-locked salmon, and a number of good trout-ponds can easily be made accessible from that point. The Lake House has accommodations for twenty-five guests, at reasonable rates, and its proprietor can furnish parties with canoes or boats and food for camping. Ship Pond Stream is impassable for canoes, and at present there is no road along either of

its banks. Parties can most comfortably go to Ship
Pond by way of Wilson Stream and Grindstone Pond,
some six or seven miles, the road thither being good
enough for teams. Ship Pond surpasses Sebec Lake
in the beauty of its situation and scenery.

The largest Buttermilk Pond is reached by a road
perhaps a mile and a half long, which leaves Buck's
Cove east of Ship Pond Stream. A road also leads
from Ship Pond, a mile and a quarter, to Big Benson
Pond, and thence down to the north shore of Buttermilk Pond. The stream which is the outlet of Benson
ponds is by some persons said to flow into Ship Pond,
and by others into Ship Pond Stream. Good fishing
is to be had at almost all seasons, both in Ship Pond
and in many of the smaller ponds near it, and both
deer and caribou are plenty in the neighborhood.

MOUNT KATAHDIN FROM THE EAST.

If one is fonder of "tramping" through the woods,
than of gliding over lakes and down streams in a canoe,
there is a route, other than that already described, by
which the ascent of Mount Katahdin can be made.

One goes by the European and North American
Railway from Bangor to Mattawamkeag, where the
cars connect with good stage-coaches for Sherman
Village, some twenty-four miles away to the north.
The stage-fare is two dollars, and the drive is a very
pleasant one, and not very tiresome. At Sherman Village one can put up at the tavern, or, if early enough,

push on by private conveyance, over a good road, six miles to Stacyville. At this place one can put up at the house of Mr. Mitchell.

It is six miles, over a rough wagon-road, from here to the East Branch of the Penobscot, where there is a house at which canoes and guides can be obtained. At Stacyville it may be well to hire a horse to carry one's load in to Katahdin Lake.

The road — an old tote-road from here — crosses the East Branch a mile below the mouth of Wassataquoik Stream, crosses the latter not far from its mouth, and runs up its north, or left, bank for seven or eight miles. The scenery along this stream is quite wild and striking. Recrossing it, the road runs westerly, five or six miles, to Katahdin Lake, from which a magnificent view is had of the mountain in all its majesty. The best place to camp is at the head of the lake, — a mile from the outlet, — at Reed's old lumber-camp on Sandy Stream.

From here to the Basin, or "crater," is about six miles. The path runs up Sandy Stream past several dams, crosses it at a long dam, and becomes quite good, until one is near the Basin, when the climbing grows difficult.

The wildest part of Katahdin scenery is had from this neighborhood, and a better idea of its grandeur and stupendous magnitude is obtained here, than from any other point. Almost surrounded by perpendicular walls of rock, the tourist never ceases to wonder at what is before him.

Good fishing is found in Katahdin Lake and Sandy Stream, and trout have been taken from the Basin pond.

FORKS OF THE KENNEBEC AND VICINITY.

FIRST ROUTE.

NORTH ANSON.

ANOTHER way of reaching Moosehead Lake and the head-waters of the Kennebec is by way of Skowhegan, or North Anson, and thence up the Kennebec valley.

The tourist leaves Boston at 7 : 30 A. M. by the Eastern, or by the Boston and Maine Railroad, and, connecting at Portland with the Maine Central Railroad, continues by way of Lewiston and Auburn to West Waterville. At this place those who wish can connect with the Somerset Railroad, and go to North Anson, or one can without change of cars continue to Skowhegan.

By the former route one crosses the Kennebec at Norridgewock, an interesting old town on its banks, which was settled early in the eighteenth century. A short distance above it the cars pass, on the left, a granite obelisk erected to Father Rasles and the Norridgewock Indians, who were slaughtered there in 1724. The pious father had come from Canada, a missionary to this wild tribe, and had succeeded in gaining a great ascendency over them. At his instigation they committed depredations on the settlers near by, at the time when the French and English were not on very good terms. Finally, Captains Harmon and Moulton were sent with two companies of soldiers to punish them. Coming on to the high ground east of their village, they divided the party, surrounded the unsuspecting Indians, and, after a brief resistance, killed most of them, and burned their chapel and village.

The railroad runs along and near the left bank of the river, crosses to the right bank at Madison, where there is quite a waterfall, and continues on the same side to North Anson. It takes about an hour and a quarter to go from West Waterville to North Anson, and the fare is one dollar.

North Anson, at the junction of the Kennebec and Carabassett Rivers, is a thriving little village, and at present the northern terminus of the Somerset Railroad. It lies on both sides of the Carabassett, a stream which runs noisily through it, over rapids of considerable length and interest. From the village a fine view is had of Mount Abraham and Mount Bigelow, to the west. The cars arrive here about half past five, and the tourist can have supper, and push on, the same evening, seven miles, to Solon, or he can stop here over night and leave for Solon the next morning at half past seven. It is forty miles from here to the Forks, the junction of Dead River with the Kennebec, and teams connect at Solon, in the morning, with the regular stage from Skowhegan, or *vice versa* from Solon, with the morning train from North

Anson to West Waterville. The fare to Solon is fifty cents. Parties can procure, at reasonable rates, a team to carry them through to the Forks, the same night.

From North Anson a good road runs twenty-seven miles to

DEAD RIVER.

Here, at Parsons's hotel, in Dead River Village, one can get canoes and staple provisions, and go up the river eleven miles, or by land nine miles, to Flagstaff Village, which is between the pond of the same name and Dead River. Seven or eight miles up the river from Flagstaff is Eustis, a small village with a mill, above which on the north branch of Dead River one can paddle twelve miles to Chain Ponds. Only one carry, and that only twenty rods long, has to be made, about four miles above Eustis, around Ledge Falls.

From Chain Ponds one crosses the Canada line, and soon descends into Lake Megantic. This is the route taken by Arnold in his famous march to Canada in October and November of 1775, he having come up the Kennebec until opposite Carrying Place Ponds, over which he crossed to Dead River, camped some time at Flagstaff, and then proceeded up the north branch through Chain Ponds into Canada.

Below Dead River Village there are six miles of "dead" water to Long Falls, one mile to the west of which is Long Pond, a good fishing-ground. In fact, the whole of this Dead River region, being out of the usual range of sportsmen, affords very good trout-fishing.

Around Long Falls there is a carry of three quarters of a mile; then come six miles of "dead" water, at the foot of which are Grand Falls and a dam. Below the dam there are wild rapids for seventeen or eighteen miles, — all the way to the Forks.

SECOND ROUTE.

SKOWHEGAN.

The route through West Waterville and Waterville to Skowhegan is perhaps more convenient than the first-named, as it involves no change of cars. Skowhegan is the head-quarters of the regular and only Kennebec stage-line, and one is more likely to get a good seat in the stage there, than if one should connect with it at Solon.

The night train from Boston fails, by two hours, to connect with the stage, unless there should be at least six persons aboard who are going up the river, and who shall have previously notified the stage to await their arrival. By this plan, however, one who wishes to buy an outfit at Skowhegan has no time to do so, and for such a person the morning train from Boston is the better, provided one can afford to lose the day spent on the cars.

Skowhegan is quite an attractive place, and the falls in the Kennebec there are well worth seeing. The Turner House, a spacious hotel, is well kept and comfortable, and within pistol-shot of the depot.

The stage leaves the hotel, for the Forks, forty-six

miles away, at half past six o'clock every morning. The road up to Solon — fifteen miles — runs through broad and undulating country, and discloses now and then pretty glimpses of distant mountains and hills. One of the prettiest views is from Robbins Hill, ten miles from Skowhegan. Moxie Mountain stands out prominently, to the north.

From Solon the road follows the course of the river up its left bank to Bingham, eight miles beyond, where stage-passengers dine. This is the terminus of the telegraph-line.

Above Bingham the hills which flank the river approach it more nearly, and the road winds around its pretty curves, now through stretches of woodland, and again through "dugways," on the very edge of the bank. It is comparatively level all of the way to the Forks, and in good weather the entire distance through Solon, Bingham, Moscow, Carratunk, and the Forks Plantation, is made in about ten hours, stops included.

Between Skowhegan and the Forks a stage runs each way every day. From the Forks to Hilton's, in Sandy Bay township, a stage runs every Tuesday, Thursday, and Saturday, arriving at Moose River Village at three o'clock P. M., and at Hilton's, fourteen miles beyond, the same evening. The stage returns on the alternate days of the week. Should the amount of travel render it expedient, the proprietors are ready to run a stage every day over this route, both ways. Passengers to Canada connect at Hilton's with the Canada stage down the Rivière du Loup to St. Joseph, thence they go by rail to Quebec.

From Solon a stage runs every morning, and connects with the cars at North Anson, at 7:45 A.M. The stage from the Forks reaches Skowhegan in the evening, in time, if required, to catch the night train for Boston. Excursion tickets from Boston to the Forks and back, by this route, cost fourteen dollars.

THE FORKS OF THE KENNEBEC

has long been a favorite resort for fishermen. A well-kept and commodious hotel is prettily and conveniently located in the centre of a large tract of fine trout-country, and the smaller game of the woods abounds in its vicinity. One of the best fishing-grounds near at hand is

MOXIE POND,

which is between ten and twelve miles long, and from a mile to a mile and a half broad. Two roads lead to it from the Forks, one on either side of Moxie Stream. That on the south side is five miles long, and the more direct; the other is two miles longer, and passes near Moxie Falls, a cascade ninety-five feet high, which should by all means be visited. Both roads come together at the dam which is at the outlet of the pond. Moxie Stream is "dead" from its mouth almost up to the falls, sixty rods above which is another fall of fifteen feet, called Rankin's Falls. From the latter point to the lower dam it is a hundred rods. Two miles intervene between the lower and upper dams, three fourths of which is 'dead" water. At the lower dam there is a farm and a very neat cabin, kept by Tom Morris; at the upper dam Frank Heald has a camp.

MOXIE FALLS.

Going up the pond one comes, at the end of a mile and a quarter, to Caribou Narrows, a charming spot for camping. Tall pines stand out above their forest companions, and with the mountains and rocks look wild and weird. Black Narrows are two and a half miles further up the pond, and Mosquito Narrows about two miles beyond them. A canoe can run up Mosquito Stream to Mosquito Pond.

Bald Rock is a mile above Mosquito Narrows, just opposite Sandy Stream, which is navigable for about a mile from its mouth. Baker Brook empties into the pond at its head, and is unnavigable. The Devil's Table, nine miles up the pond, is a large flat rock in the middle of the water. For two or three miles the upper part of the pond is narrow, and boulders and sharp rocks lie concealed just below the surface of the water.

Good fishing is to be had in Mosquito, Sandy, and Alder Brooks. Cranberries and blueberries grow in profusion on the shores of the pond, and deer and caribou are frequently seen near it.

Nine miles below the Forks a good road leads from the Kennebec, three miles, to

PLEASANT POND,

where there is quite a settlement. The water of this pond is deep and clear, so clear that one can fish successfully until quite late at night. The trout in it are of a peculiar kind, very silvery, round, plump, and delicious eating. The road continues from the north end of the pond four miles to Mosquito Pond.

Carrying-Place Ponds, and Otter and Peirce Ponds are reached from Carratunk, and are said to afford good fishing, the trout in them running as large as four and five pounds.

Fish Pond, six miles from the Forks, and two miles from the lower dam on Moxie Stream, also affords good fishing.

Black Pond, a mile from the Kennebec, has some togue in it, but few brook-trout. A convenient way of reaching Indian Pond from the Forks, by canoe, is through Black Pond, then two miles, partly by carrying, to Knight's Pond, thence one mile over a carry to Little Indian Pond, and through its boggy outlet, without serious difficulty, almost down to the mouth of Indian Stream, where some more carrying will have to be done. Elbow Bog empties into the head of Knight's Pond.

A group of ponds which furnish good fishing, and which lie pretty near together, are Wilson's Hill or Tomhegan Pond, Long Pond, above it, Horseshoe and Ellis Ponds, and the Ten-thousand-Acre Ponds. The first named is reached by going up the Canada Road three miles from the Forks, then turning to the right up the lower Cold Stream road through the Coburn field, and thence walking seven miles. A good way is to camp on the old farm on the border of Wilson's Hill Pond, and to make excursions thence, on different days, to the other ponds named, which are within a radius of two miles or less.

From the Forks to Indian Pond is fifteen miles, thence ten miles to Moosehead Lake. The better road is on the left bank of the Kennebec.

PARLIN POND.

Fifteen miles north of the Forks, on the Canada Road, is a group of buildings, — custom-house, post-office, and hotel, — which are a mile from the head of Parlin Pond, and which for many years have been a stopping-place for sportsmen. The fishing in the pond is good, and canoes and guides can be had at reasonable rates.

Five miles beyond, on the Jackman-Parlin line, is a hotel kept by A. F. Adams, the proprietor of the stage-line which runs from the Forks to Hilton's. This house is said to be very well kept, and its proprietor is attentive and obliging. It is only three miles from the foot of Parlin Pond, to which a good road runs from it. This road crosses at the dam just below the pond, and continues down the stream, and up Lang Stream to Lang Pond, where trout are abundant. Good fishing is also to be had at Parlin Pond dam. A good path runs directly from Adams's to Long Pond, — four miles.

MOOSE RIVER VILLAGE

is fifteen miles from the head of Parlin Pond, on the same Canada Road. Two small hotels flourish here, together with all the appurtenances of a well-regulated New England village. Provisions and outfit can be obtained here for a trip into the woods, but, as has been remarked elsewhere, one must not be disappointed if one does not find on the verge of the forest everything that is needed.

Leaving the village, and paddling up Moose River, one soon comes into

WOOD POND,

along whose eastern shore one goes four miles to the head of the pond. One McKinney has a farm and house here, and he can provide parties with boats, and, if need be, with a guide, too.

On the west of Wood Pond are Little Wood and Big Little Wood Ponds. The latter is half a mile from the former, and a mile wide and nearly three miles long. A good road leads from Moose River Village to the latter, and, touching it midway of its length, runs up to its head. Both ponds contain trout in abundance.

A half or three quarters of a mile of river separate Wood Pond from

ATTEAN POND,

which is rather larger than the former, and much prettier. It contains many islands, and has good shores covered with a generous amount of hard wood. From its western extremity a very good road, a mile long, runs across to Holeb Pond, and, by carrying across this one mile, one saves about twenty-seven miles of travel around the "bow."

Three miles south from the outlet of the pond

again resumes its course, and is "dead" for half a mile up to Attean Rips, just below which is a pretty little island. The carry around the "rips" is on the left, and not more than twenty rods long. There are two principal "pitches," either of which can at times be run on the setting-pole, the upper one being perhaps the more difficult.

The river is substantially smooth for eleven miles, between Attean Rips and Holeb Falls, except at Spencer Rips, three miles below the latter, and in ordinary seasons its navigation will give the canoe-man little trouble. Spencer Rips can be run on the setting-pole. At Three Brooks, opposite Bradstreet's farm, and two miles below Holeb Falls, one will get good fishing. In Town Five, near the Attean line there are two farms, one on each side of the river, but no houses.

Holeb Falls is a very picturesque spot, the water falling some twenty-five feet over large masses of rock. The carry lies on the left bank, is steep and half a mile long. A good road leaves Parlin Pond, runs west, touching at Holeb Falls, and continues up the stream to the north branch.

Above Holeb Falls, on the left, is Smith's farm, now kept by Jim Hall, — the last habitation on the river, as one goes up. The stream is substantially "dead" from this point even up to, and above, the forks of the river. It is two miles above Holeb Falls to Barrett Brook, and two and a half more to Holeb Stream. A tolerably easy passage can be had for a canoe up Holeb Stream to the pond.

Above Holeb Stream, the first brook on the right is Big Gulf Stream, and the second, — a fraction of a mile beyond, and on the same side, — Little Gulf Stream. Both are so named because of the gorges through which they flow. The mouth of Little Gulf Stream is near the town line, three quarters of a mile west of which are Lowell Falls. A short carry lies on the right bank. A short distance above the falls, on the left, is a small pond, half a mile from the river, which used to be a famous moose-ground.

So tortuous is the stream between Holeb Falls and the town line near Lowell Falls, that the distance between the two, by canoe, is about eighteen miles, while in a straight line it is less than half that number.

GAME AND FISH OF NORTHERN MAINE.

Northern Maine, like all other hunting-ground within easy reach of civilization, has been pretty thoroughly hunted and trapped, not by sportsmen, but by men who make it a business to do so. The moose, which twenty years ago roamed through its forests, and frequented the banks of its lakes and streams in large numbers, is almost extinct, and to-day it is a rare occurrence to meet one anywhere within its borders. This state of things is due to the lamentable short-sightedness of hunters, who in seasons of deep snow have, for the sake of its hide, slaughtered this noble animal by scores, and left its carcass to spoil.

An occasional moose, or other wild animal, killed by sportsmen for its meat, would scarcely be missed, and the act of killing, whether in or out of "close-time," is on this ground justified by the community. But the wanton destruction of game, by any one, for the sake of the excitement, or "sport," as it is called, will never be indulged in, nor approved, by the true sportsman.

The last remarks, *mutatis mutandis*, apply equally well to fish. The old notion has been fully disproved, that a trout once caught, would not, if put back into the water, again take a hook. Fishermen can, therefore, by undergoing a little trouble, have all the "sport" they want, and after reserving enough of their "catch" for use, return the uninjured fish to their own element.

The fish-laws of Maine have been altered and amended from year to year, to suit the fancy of each successive Legislature. None seem as yet to have hit the mark of effective protection, for it is notorious that more fish are caught in the winter and spring, when the ice first forms, and when it first breaks up, than at any other time of the year, if we except the time immediately after spawning.

As the moose disappears from Maine, deer seem to increase, and are working their way east. Caribou abound about the head-waters of the Penobscot, and apparently increase more rapidly than they are killed off. Large game is occasionally seen on the shores of Moosehead Lake. Of the fur-bearing animals, such as otter, beaver, sable, black cat, and loup-cerviers, the supply has fallen off so much, that trappers now say it does not pay to go after them.

Trout are abundant away from the beaten thoroughfares of sportsmen. In the immediate vicinity of Moosehead Lake fishing is fair at all times, except in midsummer. A hatching-house is to be built this year, near Mount Kineo, the good effect of which will in a few years be quite noticeable.

In the lake are white-fish, "lakers," and brook-trout. The first-named is very good eating, lives in deep water, and averages a pound or more in weight. The "laker," or lake-trout, weighs as high as twenty-five pounds, lives in deep water, — to the great annoyance of the white-fish, — and, in the absence of brook-trout, is deemed good eating.

The writer has not attempted to give, in these pages, exact directions as to the whereabouts of all the good fishing-pools in different ponds and streams, and for three reasons. First, and principally, he does not know where they are; secondly, they change from year to year, nay, even from day to day; and, thirdly, it would take away much pleasure from the camper-out, if he were not allowed occasionally to hunt after his game. One soon learns, without being told, that at the foot of rapids, below dams, at the mouths of cold streams, and in pools along their course, are the most likely places for fish. As to game, one should ever be ready to meet it. It comes when least expected, and may be off again before one can disengage his gun from a lot of rods and camp equipage. Keep it by your side, or in your hands, *always*, while in the woods.

Ducks are not very abundant in the interior of Maine, except in a few localities, where there are good feeding-grounds. Sheldrakes — a fishy fowl — are most common, and are found everywhere. Black ducks are numerous on the feeding-grounds, but are exceedingly shy. Teal and wood-duck are found here and there. Partridges are abundant everywhere, and are very easily approached. They are most often found along old roads, or on the banks of streams, probably because hunters do not go into the thick woods after them.

DIGEST OF THE GAME AND INLAND FISH LAWS OF MAINE.

MOOSE.

It is unlawful to take, kill, or destroy any moose, at any time, until October 1st, 1880, or thereafter, between January 1st and October 1st, in each year, under a penalty of one hundred dollars for each moose so taken, &c. Any person who aids or assists in so doing is deemed a principal. — Acts of 1878, ch. 50, §§ 1, 2.

DEER AND CARIBOU

may not lawfully be killed, taken, or destroyed between January 1st and October 1st, under a penalty of forty dollars for each one so killed, &c. — Ibid. § 4.

MOOSE, DEER, AND CARIBOU

may not lawfully be hunted with dogs, under like penalties as for killing the same. "ANY PERSON MAY LAWFULLY KILL ANY DOG FOUND HUNTING MOOSE, DEER, OR CARIBOU." — Ibid. § 4.

The possession of the hide or meat of these animals, at a time when their killing is unlawful, is presumptive, but not conclusive, evidence of having killed them. — Ibid. §§ 2, 5.

No person shall carry or transport any part of any such animals during the period in which it is unlawful to kill the same, under a penalty of forty dollars. — Ibid. § 6.

FUR-BEARING ANIMALS.

The "close-time" for mink, beaver, sable, otter, and fishers, is from May 1st to October 15th. — Ibid. § 11.

For muskrats, from June 1st to October 15th. — Acts of 1873, ch. 30, § 15.

The penalty for unlawfully taking any of the foregoing is ten dollars for each animal. — Ibid.

BIRDS.

The "close-time" for wood-duck, dusky (black) duck, or other sea-duck, is from May 1st to September 1st; for ruffed grouse (partridge), and for woodcock, from December 1st to September 1st; and for quail or pinnated grouse (prairie-chicken), from January 1st to September 1st. No one shall kill, sell, or have in possession, except alive, any of said birds, nor carry nor transport the same during the period in which their killing is prohibited, under a penalty of not less than five dollars, nor more than ten dollars for each bird. — Ibid. §§ 12, 16, as amended by ch. 126 of the Acts of 1879.

None of the above birds, nor *any* wild duck can lawfully be taken in snares or traps. Penalty, five dollars for each bird. — Ibid. § 13.

The wanton taking, or destruction, of the eggs or unfledged young of any wild bird, except of crows, hawks, or owls, is punishable by a fine of from one to ten dollars for each nest-egg or young so taken or destroyed.—Ibid. § 15.

Chapter 50 of the Acts of 1878 does not apply either to commissioned taxidermists, or to the shooting of ducks on the sea-coast. — Ibid. §§ 17, 19.

FISH.

The "close-time" for land-locked salmon, trout, and togue is from October 1st to May 1st (except on the St. Croix River and its tributaries, and on all the waters in Kennebec County, where it extends from September 15th to May 1st); for black bass, Oswego bass, and white

---

* "Killing quail is prohibited *in toto* until Sept. 1, 1883. — Ch. 189, Acts of 1880."

perch, from April 1st to July 1st. — Acts of 1878, ch. 75, § 13, as amended by ch. 122 of the Acts of 1879.

The penalty attached to the foregoing section is not less than ten dollars, nor more than thirty dollars, and a further fine of one dollar for each fish taken. In February, March, and April, however, citizens of Maine may "fish for and take land-locked salmon, trout, and togue, and convey the same to their own homes." — Ibid. § 15, as amended by ch. 122 of the Acts of 1879.

The use of grapnel, spear, trawl, weir, net, seine, trap, set-line, and spoon, either through the ice or otherwise, is prohibited. Only hand-fishing, with a single-baited hook or line, or with artificial flies, is legal. The penalty for disregarding this section is the same as that of section 15, and all grapnels, etc. are forfeited if found in use or operation, any person being authorized in such case to destroy them. — Ibid. § 14.

No person shall sell, expose for sale, or have in possession with intent to sell, or transport from place to place, within the State, any of the above fish during the period in which the taking of said fish is prohibited. All such shall be deemed to have killed, caught, or transported the same contrary to law, and be liable to the penalties provided. Penalty from ten dollars to fifty dollars. — Ibid. §§ 16, 17, as amended by ch. 122, Acts of 1879.

"No person shall fish in that portion of a pond, or other water, in which fish are artificially cultivated or maintained by the written permission of the fish-commissioners, without the permission of the proprietor, under a penalty of not less than ten nor more than one hundred dollars, and an additional penalty of two dollars for each fish so taken or killed." — Ibid. § 24.

The "close-time" for salmon is from July 15 to April 1, but between July 15 and Sept. 15 they may be taken "by the ordinary mode, with rod and single line, but not otherwise." — Ibid. § 10, as amended by ch. 187, Acts of 1880.

TOURS FOR CAMPERS.

THE following tables will show approximately the time needed to make several of the more usual tours, around and near Moosehead Lake. The night passed on the cars from Boston to Bangor is not reckoned in the tables, so that the "third night" means the night of the third *day* from Boston.

One must needs be on the move pretty much all the time, to carry out the programme laid down, and it may be well to add two or three days, in fourteen, for wet weather and other drawbacks. The enjoyment and comfort of campers will be greatly enhanced if they take half as much time again for each tour as is here thought necessary.

No. I. — ONE WEEK.

MOOSEHEAD LAKE.

Boston to Mount Kineo	1 day.
Head of lake and return	1 day.
Socatean River	1 day.
East Outlet	1 day.
Brassua Lake	2 days.
Mount Kineo to Boston	1 day.
	7 days.

No. II. — Two Weeks.

MOOSEHEAD LAKE AND VICINITY.

Boston to Mount Kineo	1 day.
Mount Kineo House	1 day.
Brassua Lake	2 days.
Tomhegan and Socatean Streams	2 days.
Mount Kineo House	1 day.
Spencer Pond	2 days.
East Outlet	2 days.
Greenville	1 day.
Wilson Pond	1 day.
Greenville to Boston	1 day.
	14 days.

No. III. — Two Weeks.

UP THE WEST BRANCH OF THE PENOBSCOT.

Boston to Mount Kineo	1 day.
Nelhudus Stream, or Seeboomook Falls	2 days.
To Forks of West Branch	1 day.
To Hale Brook	1 day.
Hale and Alder Brooks	3 days.
To Penobscot Brook (?)	1 day.
Back to Canada Falls	1 day.
To Gulliver Falls	1 day.
To Northwest. Carry	1 day.
To Kineo	1 day.
To Boston	1 day.
	14 days.

No. IV. — Two Weeks.

DOWN THE WEST BRANCH OF THE PENOBSCOT.

Boston to Moosehead Lake	1st day.
Greenville or Mt. Kineo to Moosehorn Str.	2d day.

TOURS FOR CAMPERS.

Weymouth Point, — Chesuncook Lake	3d night.
Ripogenus Carry	4th night.
Sourdnahunk Dead-Water	6th night.
Sandy Stream, — Foot of Mt. Katahdin	8th night.
Sandy Stream	9th night.
Ambajejus Lake	10th night.
Fowler's, or Medway	11th night.
Mattawamkeag	12th night.
Boston	14th day.

No. V. — Two Weeks.

DOWN THE ST. JOHN RIVER.

Boston to Moosehead Lake	1st day.
Moosehead Lake to Moosehorn Stream	2d day.
Umbazooksus Lake	3d night.
Chamberlain Lock	4th night.
Thoroughfare Brook, or Chase's Carry	6th night.
Umsaskis Lake, or Long Lake	8th night.
Allagash Falls	9th night.
Madawaska	11th night.
Grand Falls	12th night.
Woodstock	13th night.
Boston	15th day.

No. VI. — Fifteen Days.

CAUCOMGOMOC LAKE.

Boston to Moosehead Lake	1st day.
Moosehead Lake to Moosehorn Stream	2d day.
Lower Falls, — Caucomgomoc Stream	3d night.
Caucomgomoc Lake	4th night.
Avery Brook	5th night.
Round Pond	6th night.
Poland Pond	1 day.
Daggett Pond and Shallow Lake	1 day.
Allagash Lake and return to Round Pond	3 days.

Caucomgomoc Stream	12th night.
Moosehorn Stream	13th night.
Mount Kineo House.	14th night.
Boston.	16th day.

No. VII.— Two and a half to Three Weeks.

FORKS AND MOOSE RIVER.

Boston to the Forks	1 day.
The Forks	3 days.
Jackman House	2 days.
Moose River Village.	7th night.
Holeb Falls	9th night.
Lowell Falls	11th night.
Attean Pond, via Holeb Pond	13th night.
Moose River Village.	14th night.
The Forks	15th night.
Boston	17th day.
Moosehead Lake	17th night.
Boston	22d day.

THE following table gives the approximate expense of making each of the foregoing excursions from, or in the vicinity of Moosehead Lake, with one guide, and one or two tourists to a canoe. Under "R. R. Fares," there is included, in Tours 4, 5, and 7, besides meals and sleeping-car berths, the cost of transporting guide and canoe from the end of the journey back to his home.

The car-fare from Boston to Mount Kineo is $8.50; to Mattawamkeag, $8.40, — limited $7.40; and to Woodstock, $10.00.

No. of Tour	Tours	Duration of Tour	Tourists	R.R. Fares, incl. Meals & Sleeping-Cars	M. H. Lake Steamer, Passengers & Canoe	Hotels	Guide	Provisions	Carries	Total Expense. One Person	Total Expense. Two Persons
1	Moosehead Lake	One week	1 / 2	$21.00 / 42.00	$5.00 / ...	$5.00 / 10.00	$9.00	$4.00 / 6.00		$39.00	$67.00
2	Moosehead Lake & Vicinity	Two weeks	1 / 3	21.00 / 42.00		7.50 / 15.00	22.50	8.00 / 12.00		59.00	91.50
3	Up W. Branch Penobscot	Two weeks	1 / 2	21.00 / 42.00	$3.00 / 4.00	5.00 / 10.00	36.00	12.00 / 18.00	$4.00	81.00	114.00
4	Down W. Branch Penobscot	Two weeks	1 / 2	22.00 / 39.80	3.00 / 4.00	5.00 / 10.00	39.00	12.00 / 18.00	3.50	85.40	114.30
5	Down St. John River	Two weeks	1 / 2	32.50 / 57.00	3.00 / 4.00	5.00 / 10.00	42.00	12.00 / 18.00	3.00	97.50	134.00
6	Caucomgomoc Lake	15 days	1 / 2	21.00 / 42.00	6.00 / 8.00	4.00 / 8.00	35.00	12.00 / 18.00	3.00	81.00	114.00
7	Moose River	2½–3 weeks	1 / 2	34.00 / 59.00		15.00 / 30.00	25.00	12.00 / 18.00		86.00	132.00

INDEX.

	PAGE
Abacotnetic Bog	87, 88, 89, 92, 93
Abbot	112, 113
Aboljackomegus Falls	73
„ Stream	71, 73
Accidents	29, 30
Adams's House	125
Advertisements	140
Alder Brook	83, 85, 136
Alder Ground	55, 88, 89
Allagash Falls	105, 107, 137
„ Lake	99, 100, 137
„ Pond	101
„ River	93, 101, 106, 107
„ Stream	100, 101
Ambajejus Falls	74, 75, 76
„ Lake	74, 77, 137
Ambajemackomus Carry	70, 75
Arches	69, 70
Arnold	119
Aroostook River	104
Ascent of Mt. Katahdin	71
„ „ Kineo	49
Attean Pond	126, 138
„ Rips	127
Auburn	117
Avery Brook	95, 96, 137
„ Pond	95, 99
B Pond	111
Babel Brook	112
Baker Bog	92
Baker Brook	59, 92, 123
„ Lake	92, 93
„ Stream	92
Bald Brook	84
„ Mountain	86
„ Rock	123
Bangor	39, 40, 75, 106, 135
„ and Piscataquis R. R.	40, 109, 112
Barrett Brook	127
Big Benson Pond	115
„ Gulf Stream	128
„ Gull Rock	52
„ Heater	69

	PAGE
Big Island	62, 81
„ Lane Brook	86
„ Little Wood Pond	126
Bigelow, Mount	118
Bingham	121
Birch Mountain	114
„ Point	52
Black Narrows	123
„ Pond	94, 124
„ River Rapids	93
Blanchard	39, 40, 41
Blethen Landing	113
Bodfish Falls	54
Bog Brook	83, 123
Boston	39, 40, 106, 120, 122, 135, 136, 137, 138
Boston & Maine R. R.	39, 117
Bradstreet's Farm	127
Brandy Brook	94
Brassua Lake	55, 135, 136
„ Stream	56
Brownville	109, 111
Buck's Cove	114
Buoy	52
Burnt Jacket	45
Buttermilk Pond	115
Camp-fire	24
Camp-ground	22, 23
Camp "Kit"	4, 5, 6, 7
„ ornamentation	23, 24
„ Pocahontas	80
Canada	78, 117, 119, 121
Canada Falls	78, 82, 85, 136
„ Road	57, 124, 125
Canoes	16, 17, 18, 19
Capen's Landing	45, 48
Carabassett River	118
Caribou Lake	65
„ Narrows	123
„ Stream	65
Carratunk	121, 124
Carry Brook	77
„ Pond	69, 70
Carrying-Place Ponds	119, 124

	PAGE
Caucomgomoc Lake	93, 94, 95, 96, 99, 100, 137
" River	94, 101, 137, 138
Caucomgomocsis	96
Cedar Mountain	112
" Ponds	112
Centre Island	59
Chain Ponds	119
Chairback Mountain	111
" Ponds	111
Chamberlain Farm	102
" Lake	93, 98, 101, 102, 105, 107
" Lock	103, 107, 137
Chase's Carry	105, 107, 137
" Dam	104
Chemquasabamticook Lake	101
Chesuncook Dam	66, 75
" Lake	47, 62, 64, 65, 66, 67, 75, 93, 94, 99, 100, 101, 137
Churchill Lake	104
" Stream	46, 55
Cliff Beach	49, 52
Climbing	30
Coburn Farm	57
" Field	124
Colds	32, 33, 34
Cold Stream	124
Cooking	25, 26, 27
Cowen's Cove	52
Crawford Pond	112
Cuxabexis Lake	65
Daggett Pond	97, 98, 99, 137
Dam Pitch	79
Davis's	46
Day-Dream	54
Dead River	118, 119
" Village	119
Debsconeak	73
Deer Island	45, 48
Depot Farm	105
Devil's Blow-Hole	59
" Delight	52
" Elbow	105
" Table	123
Dole Brook	87, 88, 89, 91
" Falls	89, 91
Dole Pond	90, 91
" Storehouse	90, 91
Dover	41
Dressing Game	28, 29
Duck Cove	58
" Pond	65
Ducks	131

	PAGE
Eagle Lake	103
" Narrows	104
Eagle Stream	43
East Branch Penobscot	75, 103, 107, 109, 116
" Cove	41
" Outlet	45, 135, 136
Eastern R. R.	39, 117
Ebeeme Mountains	41
" Ponds	109, 110, 112
Elbow Bog	124
Ellis Pond	124
Elm Pond	79
" Stream	79
European & N. A. Railway	39, 40, 115
Eustis Village	119
Eveleth House	42
Expenses	5, 139
Farm Island	59
Fatigue	34, 35
Female Pond	77
Fish	129
" Laws	130, 133, 134
" Pond	124
Fishing Tackle	13, 53
Fitzgerald Pond	43
Flagstaff Village	119
Florenceville	106
Forks of Kennebec	117–125, 138
" of West Branch	136
" Plantation	121
Fort Kent	106
Fowler's Carry	75, 137
Foxcroft	112, 113
Fox Hole	62, 64
Fredericton	106
Frost Brook	66
" Pond	68, 90, 91
Game	129
" Laws	132, 133
Gauntlet	112
Gerrish Pond	43
Gold Mine	52
Grand Falls	75, 105, 106, 107, 109, 120, 137
" Lake	108, 109
Granite Mountain	114
Green Mountains	87, 88
Greenville	40–44, 46, 53, 107, 136
Grindstone Falls	109
" Pond	114, 115
Guides	19, 20, 21
Gulf	111, 112
Gull Rock	52

INDEX.

		PAGE
Gulliver Falls		80, 81, 136
,, Pitch		70
,, Stream		80
Guns		13, 19
Hale Brook		83, 84, 136
Hard Scrabble		49
Harrington Lake		67, 68
,, Stream		67
Hatheway's		65
Haymock Lake		103
Heater		69
High Landing		87, 88
Hilton's		121, 125
Hog Back Island		48
Holeb Falls		127, 128, 138
,, Pond		126, 138
,, Stream		127, 128
Horace Falls		110, 112
Horseback Mountain		111
Horseshoe Pond		110, 124
Hotels	42, 46, 51, 61, 65, 111, 113, 114, 116, 119, 120, 122, 125, 139
Houston Dead-Water		111
,, Ponds		111
Hunger		34, 35
Hurd Ponds		96
Hygienic Notes		29 et seq.
Indian Pond	45, 46, 54, 55, 124, 125
,, Stream		124
Island Falls		67
Jackman		125, 138
Johnson's Landing		43
Jo Mary Lakes		76, 109, 112
,, Road		109, 110, 112
Katahdin. — See Mt. Katahdin.		
,, Iron-Works		47, 109, 111
,, Lake		116
,, Pond		73
Katepskonegan Dead-Water		73
Kennebec	41, 45, 52, 117-120, 123-125
,, Dam		45
Kineo. — See Mt. Kineo.		
,, Bay		49
,, Point		49
King's High Landing		81
Kinneho		50
Knight's Pond		124
Knights's Farm		81
Lake House		42, 114
,, Megantic		119
Lane's Clearing		78, 81
Lang Pond		125
,, Stream		125

		PAGE
Leadbetter Brook		86
,, Falls		87, 89
Ledge Falls		119
Legend		50
Lewiston		117
Lily Bay		46
,, Mountains		41
Liquors		12, 35, 36, 37
Little Brassua Pond		56, 57
,, Gulf Stream		128
,, Gull Rock		52
,, Heater		69
,, Indian Pond		124
,, Kineo		48
,, Pleasant Pond		47
,, Scott Brook		94
,, Spencer Pond		47
,, Wood Pond		126
Lobster Lake		64
,, Stream		62, 63
Long Falls		119, 120
,, Lake	93, 101, 105, 107, 137
,, Pond	57, 91, 111, 119, 124, 125
Loon Lake		96, 99
Lowell Falls		128, 138
Lucky Pond		48
Luggage		7-13
Madawaska		137
,, River		106, 107
Madison		118
Maine Central R. R.		39, 117
Maquaso		50
Mattawamkeag	75, 76, 109, 115, 137
		138
McKinney's Farm		126
Medway		109, 137
Megantic Lake		119
Miasm		31
Middle Branch		89
Millinokett Lake		73, 77
,, Stream		75
Milo		40, 109
Miseree Stream		55
Moody Islands		48, 53
Moose Brook		59, 65
Moosehead Lake	39-41, 44, 50, 57, 61, 77, 117, 125, 130, 135-138
Moosehorn Stream	62, 64, 107, 136, 137, 138
Moose Pond		65
,, River	45, 52, 55, 56, 57, 126, 127
,, ,, Bridge		57
,, ,, Village	121, 125, 138
Morris Farm		61, 62, 64, 79
Moscow		121

INDEX.

	PAGE
Mosquito Narrows	123
,, Pond	123
,, Repellent	12
,, Stream	123
Mount Abraham	118
,, Bigelow	118
,, Katahdin	40, 63, 64, 66, 68, 69, 71, 73, 75, 77, 115, 116, 137
,, Kineo	44, 45, 48, 53, 55, 57-59, 64, 107, 130, 135, 136, 138
,, Kineo House	49, 51, 53, 54, 136, 138
Moxie Falls	122
,, Mountain	121
,, Pond	122
,, Stream	122
Mud Pond	93, 101, 102
,, Carry	102
Mummer-Nunner-Lungen Pond	111
Munsungan Lake	104
Murphy's Farm	94
Muskrat Pond	77
Mystic Grotto	52
Nahmakanta Lake	76, 77
Nelhudus Stream	80, 81, 136
New Brunswick	103
Norridgewock	117
Norris Brook	88, 89
North Anson	117-119, 122
North Brook	46
,, Branch	81, 85, 86, 88, 90, 91
,, Twin Dam	74, 76
,, ,, Lake	74
Northeast Carry	58, 59, 61, 78, 79
Northwest Carry	59, 77-79, 136
Norton's Farm	110
Number in Party	2
Old Canada Road	78, 80, 82, 83, 84
Oldtown	39, 40
Ore Mountain	111
Otter Pond	124
Outfit	3, 4
Pack-straps	11
Paddling	16
Pamedomcook Lake	74, 76
Parlin Pond	125, 127
Partridges	131
Party	2
Passamagamock Falls	74
Pearl Pond	110
Pebble Beach	49, 52
Peirce Ponds	124
Penobscot	41, 50, 61, 64, 68, 79
,, Brook	84, 85, 136

	PAGE
Penobscot Lake	84
,, Pond	77
Personal Luggage	7-13
Pine Mountain	114
,, Stream Falls	62, 63, 64
Piscataquis	40
Pleasant Pond	123
,, River	109-113
Pocahontas Camp	80
Pockwockamus Dead-Water	73
,, Falls	73
Poland Brook	97, 98
,, Pond	98, 99, 137
Poling	17
Pollywog Pond	77
Pomolah Mountain	73
Posture in Canoe	17, 18
Portland	106
Profile	50
Provisions	14, 15, 16
Putting-in Place	69
Quakish Lake	74
Quebec	121
Quicksands	31
Ragmuff Stream	62
Rainbow Lake	76, 77
Rankin's Falls	122
Rasles, Father	117
Recipes	25, 26, 27
Ripogenus Carry	69, 75, 137
,, Gorge	68
,, Lake	66-69
Rivière du Loup	121
Roach Pond	46, 47
,, River	46
Robbins Hill	121
Robert Brook	90
Rocky Rips	62, 63
Rolling Dam Ledge	57
Round Pond	53, 96, 99, 137
Routes	39, 40, 115, 117, 120
Russell Brook	104
,, Mountain	40
,, Pond	79
,, Stream	79
Sam's Pitch	55
Sand Bar	48
,, Island	48
Sandy Bay	84, 121
,, Stream	71, 73, 75
Schoodic Lake	109, 110
Sears's Clearing	62
Season	1, 2
Sebec Corner	112

	PAGE
Sebec Lake	112, 113, 115
„ Village	112, 113
Second Lake	108
Seeboomook Falls	78, 79, 136
„ Island	78, 79
„ Meadows	78
„ Stream	79, 81
Seven Islands	93, 105
Shad Pond	75, 76
Shallow Lake	97–99, 137
Sherman Village	115, 116
Ship Pond	115
„ Stream	114, 115
Shirley	41
Skinning Game	28
Skowhegan	117, 118, 120, 121
Slate Mountain	114
Slaughter Pond	68
Smith Brook	103
Smith's Farm	127
Snare Brook	104
Socatean Falls	58
„ Point	59
„ Pool	58
„ River	58, 135, 136
Solon	118, 120, 121
Somerset R. R.	117, 118
Soper Brook	67, 104
Sourdnahunk Carry	71
„ Dead-Water	70, 71, 137
„ Lake	67
„ Mountains	66
„ Stream	67, 71
South Branch Penobscot	81, 82, 85, 86
South Lagrange	40
„ Sebec	112
Spencer Bay	45, 46, 47
„ Brook	46. 47
„ Mountains	47, 64
„ Pond	47, 136
„ Rips	127
Spencer's Camp	87–89
Spider Lake	104
Spruce Mountain Pond	111
Square Lake	105
Squaw Brook	43
„ Mountain	41
„ Pond	43
Stacyville	116
Steamboats	44, 54
Stimulation	12, 35–57
St. John	50, 106
„ Pond	89, 91–93
„ River	93, 137
St. Joseph	121

	PAGE
Stony Brook Rapids	57
Store	53
Sugar Island	45, 50
Summit of Katahdin	72
Sun-stroke	34
Swan's Farm	80, 81
Swimming	30
Table-Land	72
Table Rock	49
Taking Cold	32–34
Telos Lake	103, 107
Telosmis	107
Ten-thousand Acre Ponds	124
Tent	6, 22, 23
Thoroughfare Brook	104, 107, 137
Three Brooks	127
„ Sisters	49, 50, 52
Tobique	106
Tom Fletcher Brook	56
Tomhegan Pond	124
„ River	57, 58, 136
Toulbah Mountains	100
Tours	135, 139
Traveller Mountains	108
Trout Brook	108
Truesdell's Camp	88, 89
Twin Brooks	104
Umbazooksus Lake	102, 107, 137
„ Stream	93. 101
Umsaskis Lake	105, 107, 137
Uncle Jim's Carry	114
Upper Dam, — South Branch	85
Wadleigh Brook	67, 99
„ Pond	77
Wangen Brook	110
Wassataquoik Mountain	73
„ Stream	116
Waterville	120
Webster Brook	108
„ Lake	103, 107, 108
West Branch Penobscot	62–64, 68, 75, 78, 109, 136
„ Cove	43
„ Outlet Stream	46, 54
„ Waterville	117–120
Weymouth Point	65, 137
Williams Stream	59
Wilson Ponds	42, 43, 136
„ Stream	113–115
Wilson's Hill Pond	124
Woboostook Stream	92
Wood	24, 25
„ Pond	57. 126
Woodstock	106, 107, 137, 138

IF YOU ARE GOING

TO

Moosehead Lake, Rangeley Lake, Mount Desert, Poland Springs, Boothbay, Castine, Eastport, Bethel, Andover, Gorham, Bridgeton, Mount Pleasant, or to any other point in the STATE OF MAINE,

YOU WILL FIND THE MOST CONVENIENT ROUTE VIA

THE EASTERN RAILROAD.

It is also the Shortest and ONLY LINE WITHOUT CHANGE OF CARS from Boston to Crawford and Fabyan's, through the White Mountain Notch,

And for Wolfboro', Intervale, North Conway, Glen House, Bethlehem, Profile, and Jefferson. Swampscott, Marblehead, Manchester-by-the-Sea, Magnolia, Gloucester, Rockport, Pigeon Cove, Salisbury, Rye and Hampton Beaches, Plum Island, Isles of Shoals, Old York and Newcastle, are reached only by this route.

PULLMAN PALACE CARS

On day trains, Boston and Portland; and **SLEEPING CARS**, Boston and Bangor, on night trains.

Observation and Palace Cars on White Mountain Trains.

Through and Excursion Tickets on sale at all principal Offices.

☞ Send for Excursion List and Summer Time Table.

City Office, 306 Washington Street, Boston.
DEPOT IN BOSTON, ON CAUSEWAY STREET.

D. W. SANBORN,
    Master of Transportation.

LUCIUS TUTTLE,
    G. P. & T. Agent.

THE MAINE CENTRAL RAILROAD

Is the great Railway Thoroughfare of the State, and forms, with its own line and branches, the only rail route between

PORTLAND AND BANGOR,

Brunswick, Bath, Richmond, Gardiner, Augusta, Skowhegan, Waterville, Belfast, Dexter, and Farmington, and is the best and most direct route to **AUBURN AND LEWISTON**, and all parts of the State of Maine. It connects with all trains from and to New York, Boston, Worcester, Rockland, Houlton, Woodstock, Fort Fairfield, Caribou, St. Stephen, Fredericton, and is the most important link in the line between

BOSTON, ST. JOHN, AND HALIFAX.

It offers the best facilities for reaching all of the resorts of Maine east of Portland, and is the only route whereby

MOOSEHEAD LAKE,

With its beautiful scenery, delightful sailing, and excellent fishing and hunting, may surely be reached the day following departure from Boston.

THE ROUTE From Boston is *via* morning trains of Boston & Maine or Eastern Railroads, and from other points *via* any route to Portland, thence by noon train of Maine Central Railroad to Bangor, and stop over night; or take the Night Express Train, with Pullman Sleeping Cars attached, leaving Eastern Railroad Depot at 7 P.M., and Portland soon after 11, arriving in Bangor about 6 the following morning, connecting with Bangor and Piscataquis Railroad for the Lake.

EXCURSION TICKETS From New York are sold by all of the Sound Lines, and from Providence, Worcester, and Nashua by the W. & N. R. R.

FARES.

From Boston to Mt. Kineo House and Return $15.00
Portland, Brunswick, Bath, and Lewiston 12.00
Gardiner . . . . . $10.50.   Augusta and Belfast . 10.00

OTHER RESORTS IN THE
WILDERNESS OF NORTHERN MAINE

ARE REACHED, VIA THIS LINE, AS FOLLOWS:

THE RANGELEY LAKES, via Farmington and Phillips.
DEAD RIVER, via North Anson.
THE FORKS OF THE KENNEBEC, via Skowhegan.
AROOSTOOK COUNTY and the Waters of the Upper **ST. JOHN**, via Fort Fairfield and Caribou, Me., Grand Falls and Edmundston, N. B.

FARES.

Boston to **Rangeley** and Return, $12.50; Portland, $9.50.
Boston to **Forks of Kennebec** and Return, via Skowhegan, $13.00; Portland, $10.00.
Boston to **Dead River** (Parson's Hotel) and Return, via North Anson, $13.00; Portland, $10.00.
Boston to **Caribou, Maine,** and Return, $18.00; Portland, $15.00.
Boston to **Edmundston, N. B.,** $20.00; Portland, $17.00.

This is also the Route to the Seaside Resorts of
MT. DESERT, CASTINE, CAMDEN, BOOTHBAY,
MOUSE AND SQUIRREL ISLANDS, &c.

And besides being the best route to the resorts already mentioned, this line runs through, or within easy distance of, numbers of picturesque and healthful villages along the sea-coast and in the interior, which, with their attractive scenery and invigorating atmosphere, are so rapidly and widely known and appreciated as *Summer Resorts,* and drawing increased numbers of visitors each year.

F. E. BOOTHBY,   PAYSON TUCKER,
General Ticket Agent.   *Superintendent.*

DAVID BUGBEE & CO.,

Booksellers and Stationers,

No. 5 Kenduskeag Bridge,

BANGOR, MAINE.

European & North American Railway,

HANNIBAL HAMLIN and WM. B. HAYFORD, *Trustees.*

INTERNATIONAL ROUTE!

THE ONLY ALL-RAIL LINE

BETWEEN THE

United States and Maritime Provinces.

THE DIRECT ROUTE TO THE

PENOBSCOT WATERS,
MOUNT KATAHDIN,

And the Fishing and Hunting Grounds

OF

NORTHERN MAINE and NEW BRUNSWICK.

EXCURSION TICKETS, to points reached *via* this Line, on sale at all Principal Ticket Offices.

The completion of the New Brunswick Railway to Edmundston brings the country of the fertile Aroostook and St. John Valleys of easy access with all parts of the United States. To the **Tourist and Sportsman,** this country offers superior advantages. Rich in natural attractions, scenery unrivalled for grandeur and beauty, streams and lakes abounding with salmon, tulade, togue, trout, and white-fish, with wild fowl in abundance, and forests stocked with game, there is no other such field for sportsmen in America east of the Rocky Mountains.

J. F. LEAVITT,	**F. W. CRAM,**
Gen'l Ticket Agent,	*Superintendent,*
Bangor, Me.	**Bangor, Me.**

Campers and Lumbermen, Attention!

A NEW AND VALUABLE INVENTION.

THE
CROSBY PATENT AXE COVER.

NO LUMBERMAN NOR CAMPER SHOULD BE WITHOUT IT.

Made of stout leather, with brass trimmings. It is cheap, light, and durable; will not rust, and protects the edge of the axe from becoming nicked or dulled, and renders it safe to carry. Also,

INDIAN HATCHETS AND AXES,

With broad steel heads, made specially for campers, and adapted for use in the woods. Three sizes.

SEND STAMP FOR CIRCULAR.

A. S. CROSBY & CO., Manufacturers,
WATERVILLE, MAINE.

BANGOR HOUSE - - - BANGOR, MAINE.

This is one of the best houses in New England; it sits in a square by itself, thus avoiding the danger of fire from other buildings, and making every room a front one. It has a brick partition between nearly every room, making it fire proof. FREE COACHES are run to and from all trains and boats. **$2.00 per day.**

F. O. BEAL, Proprietor.

N. M. JONES & CO.,
Sole Agents in MAINE for the
CONFECTIONERY
OF
JAMES DUCKWORTH AND SON,
Brooklyn, New York,
AND
STEPHEN F. WHITMAN & SONS,
PHILADELPHIA.

The finest Line of Confectionery in the State. Also,
A Full Line of Choice Valencia and Messina Oranges, Lemons, Dates, Figs, Bananas, Canned Goods, and Country Produce,
AT WHOLESALE AND RETAIL.
Special attention paid to filling Orders.

☞ Send for our Price List.

10 West Market Square, Bangor, Me.

THOS. JENNESS & SON,

JOBBERS AND RETAILERS OF

Hardware and Fine Cutlery,

PISTOLS, CARTRIDGES, FISHING TACKLE, &C.,

No. 12 West Market Square,

BANGOR, MAINE.

CHARLES DWINEL,

DEALER IN

Fine Family Stores and Fancy Groceries,

FOREIGN AND DOMESTIC GREEN AND DRY FRUITS,

OF THE FINEST QUALITY.

Sportsmen's Supplies packed in the Best and Most Convenient Manner.

Orders, by Mail or otherwise, promptly Filled and Forwarded.

NO. 3 KENDUSKEAG BRIDGE, AND 2 HARLOW ST.,

BANGOR, MAINE.

MT. KINEO HOUSE.

MEALS.

Breakfast, 7.30 *to* 9 A.M.; *Dinner*, 1½ P.M.; *Supper*, 6½ P.M.

BOARD AND LODGING.

Single person, $8.00 to $15.00 a week, according to location of room.
Man and wife, $15.00 to $25.00.
Children, usually half price.
Nurse and young child (under two years), $1.00 to $1.50 a day.
Transients, $2.00 to $2.50 a day.
Single meals, 75 cents; Lodging, 50 cents.

In July, a discount of 15 per cent is made on the above prices

BOATS.

Row-boats to let, at 50 cents a day, or $2.50 a week.
Canoes, 25 cents a day, — for long trips, less.

The "DAY-DREAM," $10.00 a day.

To Head of Lake, $10.00. To Lily Bay or Spencer Bay, $5.00.
To East Outlet, $3.00 to $4.00, — large parties, 25 cents apiece.
To Socatean or Tomhegan, $3.00 to $5.00, — according to size of party.
Around the Mountain, parties of twelve or fifteen, 25 cts. apiece.

FARES ON STEAMERS.

Greenville to Kineo, or reverse, $1.00; round trip, $1.50.
Kineo to Greenville and return, not necessarily on same day (guests of hotel), 75 cents.
Kineo to Head of Lake and return on same trip (guests of hotel), $1.00.

MOUNT KINEO

Is a magnificent promontory, situated near the middle of

Moosehead Lake,

In the State of Maine, and almost divides the Lake, as it rises from the water to a *perpendicular height of nearly* 1,200 *feet*.

THE MOUNT KINEO HOUSE

Is situated at the foot of *Mount Kineo,* in close proximity to the

FAVORITE HUNTING AND FISHING GROUNDS,

And in the midst of the

Grand and Beautiful Scenery

For which the region is famed. Nearly one thousand feet above the sea level, surrounded by the great pine-forests, and fanned by breezes passing over the clear waters of the Lake, the *Mount Kineo House* offers many inducements to those seeking refuge from the city-heats, and to

SUFFERERS FROM HAY-FEVER.

The attractions for sportsmen at this resort are too well known to need comment. Every thing required for a trip in the woods may be obtained at the house. Boats, birch-canoes, &c., are always in readiness. The elegant little steamer "*Day-Dream*" will always be available for the use of the guests of the house. Billiard-room, bowling-alleys, and croquet-grounds are convenient and in good order. For any information, address

O. A. DENNEN, Superintendent,

MOUNT KINEO HOUSE, MOOSEHEAD LAKE, ME

NEW POCKET MAP

OF

MOOSEHEAD LAKE

AND VICINITY,

Embracing the **Headwaters of the Kennebec, Penobscot, and St. John Rivers**, and giving routes for the tourist and lumber-man through the great forests, and over the intricate water-courses of

NORTHERN MAINE.

It contains the latest geographical corrections of this great expanse of wild country, and will be found serviceable by all who contemplate a visit to these secluded localities.

COMPILED AND PUBLISHED BY

LUCIUS L. HUBBARD, CAMBRIDGE, MASS.

Printed on heavy bond-paper, and encased in durable envelope to fit the pocket. **Price, 75 cents.**

Will be sent by mail, post-paid, on receipt of price,

by

A. WILLIAMS & CO., BOSTON, MASS.

D. BUGBEE & CO., BANGOR, ME.

SUMMER VACATIONS

AT

MOOSEHEAD LAKE

AND VICINITY.

A PRACTICAL GUIDE TO THE WOODS AND WATERS OF NORTHERN MAINE, ILLUSTRATED WITH VIEWS OF PENOBSCOT AND KENNEBEC SCENERY.

By LUCIUS L. HUBBARD.

FIRST EDITION. — Albertype Illustrations, and accompanied by a new and large map of the Headwaters of the Penobscot, Kennebec, and St. John Rivers. Cloth binding. $1.50.

SECOND EDITION. — Woodcut Illustrations. Small Maps. Paper. 75 cents. *Map in special envelope, 75 cents.*

Special Rates made to Railroads and Hotels.

Either of the above publications will be forwarded, post-paid, on receipt of price, by

A. WILLIAMS & CO., BOSTON, MASS.

D. BUGBEE & CO., BANGOR, ME.

WM. READ AND SONS,

13 Faneuil Hall Square, Boston,

SOLE NEW ENGLAND AGENTS FOR

COLT'S NEW BREECH LOADER.

THE BEST AMERICAN GUN!

The reputation of the Colt's Revolver Co. for highest quality in all arms of their manufacture is a sufficient recommendation for this gun. It is of the favorite top-snap, double-bolt action, with latest improvements, as Rebounding Locks, &c.

PRICE $50.00 AND UPWARDS.

Agents for W. & C. Scott & Son's celebrated Breech Loaders.

FINE TROUT AND SALMON RODS,

Flies, Lines, and every thing in Fishing Tackle, Tourists' Knapsacks, Tents, Rubber Blankets, &c., Winchester, Sharp, Maynard, and all makes of Rifles.

We now offer a lot of Sharp's Sliding-Barrel Sporting Rifles, 45 calibre, Central Fire, Reloadable Cartridge. They use the same cartridge as the Colt Revolver; and from the fact that the cartridge can be reloaded, are desirable for parties going into camp. The best low-priced Rifle in the market. Price only $13.50.

SEND STAMP FOR CIRCULARS.

THE BOSTON AND MAINE RAILROAD

Is the *POPULAR* and *RELIABLE* route to the

FISHING & HUNTING GROUNDS OF MAINE,

Making close connections at PORTLAND with Railroads and Steamship Lines for the *RANGELEY* and *MOOSEHEAD LAKES*, and the many lakes and streams of Northeastern Maine.

EXCURSION TICKETS

To the above points, and many others, among which are Glen House (White Mountains), Gorham, N.H., Bethel, Andover, Bryant's Pond, *Poland Springs, Bar Harbor* (Mount Desert), Fabyan's and Crawford's (White Mountains), Sebago Lake, and *KENNEBUNK* and

Old Orchard Beaches.

Station in Boston: Head of Washington Street, Haymarket Square.

Send for List of Excursions and Prices.

JAS. T. FURBER,   D. J. FLANDERS,
GEN. SUP'T.   GEN. TICKET AG'T.

www.ingramcontent.com/pod-product-compliance
Lightning Source LLC
Chambersburg PA
CBHW020842160426
43192CB00007B/750